10|98

23.⁶⁰

Miles Davis

George R. Crisp

Miles Davis

George R. Crisp

An Impact Biography

FRANKLIN WATTS
A Division of Grolier Publishing
New York • London • Hong Kong • Sydney
Danbury, Connecticut

For Julie

Interior Book Design by Claire Fontaine

Photographs ©: AP/Wide World Photos: 115, 123, 129; Archive Photos: 31, 40, 58, 69 (Metronome Colllection), 50; Corbis-Bettmann: 90 (Frank Driggs), 46, 95; Frank Driggs Collection: 2, 29, 36, 54, 63, 78, 82, 83, 86; Northwestern University: 18; Retna Ltd: 98 (Baron Wolman); UPI/Corbis-Bettmann: 105.

Library of Congress Cataloging-in-Publication Data
Crisp, George R.
    Miles Davis / George R. Crisp.
    p. cm. — (An impact biography)
    Discography
    Includes biographical references (p.   ) and index.
    ISBN 0-531-11319-1(lib. bdg.)   ISBN 0-531-15865-9(pbk.)
    1. Davis, Miles—Juvenile literature. 2. Jazz musicians—United States—Biog-raphy—Juvenile literature. [1. Davis, Miles. 2. Musicians. 3. Afro-Americans—Biography. 4. Jazz.] I. Title.
ML3930.D33C72   1997
788.9'2165'092—dc20

[B]   96-26427
                                                                CIP
                                                              AC MN

Contents

Acknowledgments

I would like to acknowledge for their help and support, in no particular order, Sylvester Reese, Dorothy London, Richard Lanoix, Dominique Simmoneaux, Jeff Ellenberger, and my parents and aunt.

Miles Davis

George R. Crisp

One
Coda

Summer 1991. Montreux, Switzerland. The long and winding road had come to an end. The band unpacked, the roadies hit the stage to set up the show. History of an unknown sort was about to be made.

The large, affluent-looking crowd buzzed with anticipation. Excitement permeated the crisp, clean air. People of all ages were there: new fans who had been in short pants when Miles left the scene in 1975 and older fans who had first seen Miles on his frequent European tours in the late 1950s, 1960s, and 1970s.

The older fans were a little different. They were the ones who cherished the Miles of *Workin'*; *Walkin'*; *Steamin'*; *Milestones*; *My Funny Valentine*; *Miles Smiles*; and the Miles of the Gil Evans's collaborations, such as *Porgy and Bess*, *Miles Ahead*, and *Sketches of Spain*. Although they naturally had become disenchanted when Miles went electric, they hung around. Their memories of Miles were associated with key events in their lives: postwar prosperity, perhaps, when the Americans came en masse to Europe and brought with them this wonderful music called jazz. Jazz and Miles to them meant sophistication, becoming an adult, having sex for the first time, traveling abroad, or going to the United States to see where this all began. Miles to them was an honorary European, befriended by Picasso and Sartre, the lover of the beautiful and talented French singer Juliette Greco. They thought it a pity that Miles hadn't settled down in Paris or Stockholm, as some of his colleagues—such musical gypsies as Sidney Bechet, Dexter Gordon, Bud Powell, Stan Getz, Kenny Clarke, and Eric Dolphy—had.

Miles also meant to them the arrogant, angry young man with a horn, a real SOB who turned his back on the audience, who conceded nothing to the fans, the critics, his fellow musicians, or, above all, to himself. He was an elegant survivor, the voice of pain and beauty, of sorrow suffered and endured, and joy discovered and celebrated, a wraithlike figure of strength whose surliness and acidity concealed a great generosity of spirit, kindness, and deep shyness. He was Miles the conqueror, the innovator, the great introducer and discoverer of talent, Miles the creative lover and hateful destroyer.

The older ones were miles apart from the younger revelers. To the young, Miles was the natty clean cat in Brooks Brothers suits or tailored Italian clothing, the hard bopper who underwent his jazz baptism with Fathers Bird and Diz presiding, the arrogant son of a bitch who turned his back to the audience, the surly, raspy-voiced interview, outspoken and controversial. The younger fans, on the other hand, knew little, if anything, about modal or chromatic jazz, free or cool jazz, bop or hard bop, or swing. Many of them did not know that Miles had once played acoustically. Electronics was all they knew, heard, or cared about.

Very few of them knew Miles, the honorary European,

the occasional pal of Picasso and Sartre, and lover of Juliette Greco (Who was Juliette Greco? many of them asked). Their Miles was yet a different character altogether, also elegant, still a sharp dresser, but much more affable, a pitchman for Honda motor scooters, the cool purveyor of highly sophisticated pop music. Who was Jackie McLean? Who was Walter Bishop? Who the hell was Sonny Rollins? Get them off the stage and just give us Miles—the man with the horn whose music united them all.

They gathered here in Montreux—young and old—to pay homage and to enjoy, though rumor had it that Miles was seriously ill.

All the big acts had taken the stage, played, and left. John Scofield. David Sanborn. Bill Evans (the saxophonist, not the pianist). Wallace Roney. The Modern Jazz Quartet. Eddie Gomez. Clark Terry. Robert Cray. B. B. King. Cleo Laine and John Dankworth. Herbie Mann. Jean-Luc Ponty. Jeff Ellenberger. McCoy Tyner. Pete Barbuti. Quincy Jones. And others. All of them had come to enjoy that great Swiss hospitality, the fresh mountain air, and friendly people. The weather had been perfect, as usual, and musicians and fans alike were having a blast.

But this was the last night, and as all last nights are, it was a time for reflection and rumination, maybe even a little sadness. The end was near, so they paced the final curtain. The last guest, Miles Davis himself, even without all the rumors and the theatrics of the occasion, always inspired such mixtures of strangely conflicting, intense emotions. Maybe this would be his final time at Montreux—or anywhere else for that matter.

In any event the great man had yet to make his appearance. Everyone waited. There were camera crews from all over Europe: England's BBC, Italy's RAI, Germany's Telefunken, and even a few from the United States.

Where was he? It was nearing 11 P.M.

Quincy Jones, whose pickup group, performing his latest compositions, had wowed the packed crowd, casually leaped onto the stage. Huge applause for the producer of *The Color Purple.* The band tuned up. More scattered applause, a crescendo of sound, and then Quincy spoke:

Merci. Merci, Claude. Anything can happen up here tonight, but I'd like to bring out now a man that if he never played another note he doesn't have to. He has led the way on the cutting edge for the last fifty years and it's a dream to work with him tonight for the first time. My love, my brother, and one of my favorite musicians and idols— Miles Davis!

Great applause and a standing ovation greeted Miles as he was led onto the stage by Jones. Miles clearly needed help, for he leaned on Jones for support as he was brought to the microphone. He was decked out, as was his custom, in the latest threads from Kenzo. His wraparound Ray Bans protected his eyes from the glare of the light and the blinding photo flashes.

Still the audience stood and applauded, a touching outpouring of love and respect. Musicians, former sidemen, and peers were in that appreciative audience, loudly exclaiming their feelings for the man. Miles uncharacteristically acknowledged the listeners, but without further ado he got down to business.

And then the greatest surprise yet, even greater than his unexpected appearance: he kicked off the set by playing "Boplicity," a tune that his mother, Cleota Henry Davis, had penned, and that his great friend and collaborator, the late Gil Evans, arranged for *Birth of the Cool* in 1949. It was probably the first time he played it in 40-some years. And here it was again, dusted off, good as new, movingly played, a bit shaky perhaps, but its essence shining through, the heart and soul of it all there.

A little brush, a few vamps here, a riff there, a firm bass line, the rising young star Wallace Roney's trumpet urging and helping Miles along, and the concert was off in full swing. "Boplicity." The introduction to "Miles Ahead." "Springsville." "Maids of Cadiz." "The Duke." "My Ship." "Miles Ahead." "Blues for Pablo." The introduction to "Porgy and Bess." "Orgone." "Gone, Gone, Gone." "Summertime." "Here Comes Da Honey Man." "The Pan Piper." "Solea." And then it was over.

On Saturday, October 28, 1991, almost two months after this golden flourish, Miles Davis died of everything in Los Angeles. He went down swinging.

2
The Inner Light

In the lives of each and every one of us, the great and the obscure, the high and the mighty, the low and the meek, the good, the bad, and the ugly, there is usually an incident in childhood that, to some extent, acts as a metaphor for all that follows, that sets a pattern our lives might take. There is the legendary Heracles who slew a viper in his cradle. There is David who slew Goliath, and Daniel who pacified the lions. There is also the Roman emperor Claudius who caught a wolf pup in his arms that had been dropped by an eagle.

In his autobiography, Miles speaks of a rather more mundane incident. His earliest memory was the *whoosh* of a shooting blue flame. The flame came from a gas stove, and he was playing near it at the time. Someone may have lit it, or maybe Miles did, but what mattered was that it was lit. Miles felt its heat close to his face, was startled by its suddenness.

Along with this first memory was his first feeling of

Miles Dewey Davis II poses for his Northwestern
University Dental School graduation photo.
"Doc" Davis encouraged his son, Miles, to pursue
his dream.

fear. Nothing cool in being burnt. Yet despite that feeling of fear, of nearly being burnt, Miles felt an instinctive, strong attraction to the flame, to this fiery sensation. He loved playing with fire, whether in his nocturnal wanderings, his various personal relationships, or in his music. For most of the next 60 years, he would dance around an inner burning light, like a moth around a porch light on a summer night. Fear and defiance. Love and hate. Assertion and retreat. Back and forth he would rock, like a pendulum.

If nothing else, Miles always looked ahead, never back—perhaps fearing someone might be gaining on him, but most likely not. Miles usually led the charge, in music anyway.

Miles Dewey Davis III was born in the small river town of Alton, Illinois, on May 26, 1926. The second of three children, he was named after his father, Miles Dewey Davis II, a dentist and successful businessman who, in turn, was named after his father, an accountant, successful livestock raiser, and landowner. Miles was nicknamed Junior, a moniker that he truly hated.

Miles was born into a prosperous middle-class environment, a special place that the Davises seemed almost predestined to occupy. As slaves three generations earlier, the Davises had been not in the fields but in the house, carrying out a variety of duties: accounting, cooking, acting as butlers, maids, and valets. But the most significant occupation they had held, one which reasserted itself in Miles with a vengeance, was that of musician.

After emancipation, however, the Davises turned their backs on music. It was not until Miles came along some 70 years later that a Davis once again took up music. One reason his family rejected music was that for middle-class blacks, the playing of music, especially such lowly regarded forms as honky-tonk, blues, and the then-nascent jazz (which came out of that lustful, decadent city of New

Orleans), was considered not at all reputable. It was a reminder of the bad old days of slavery, of enforced servitude. Classical music and church spirituals and hymns, however, were respectable and therefore encouraged.

Born to a prosperity that endured even into the economic depression that was just around the corner, Miles had a seemingly idyllic childhood, lacking for nothing. His father was regarded as rich for a black man of his time. He had studied dentistry at Northwestern University and provided well for his family. The family did not stay in Alton for long after Miles's birth. Doc Davis, as he was called, moved his family farther south to East St. Louis, Illinois, a meatpacking center located across the Mississippi River from St. Louis, Missouri. There, on account of Doc Davis's high-status profession and comfortable income, the Davises became pillars of the East St. Louis African-American community.

Miles's mother, Cleota Henry Davis, was a beautiful woman, partly of Indian descent. She came from a musical family; her father was an organ teacher. The Henrys, like the Davises, were middle class, but as Miles put it in his autobiography, they were a bit "uppity," a bit too self-conscious of their privileged state and not unafraid to let others know it. He never felt comfortable with them or her.

Growing up, Miles was fairly pampered. Not only did his father spoil him, but so too did the neighborhood, which was integrated. Miles grew up among children of many different racial and ethnic backgrounds, particularly German, Jewish, Armenian, and Greek. One of his earliest friends was a Greek-American boy named Leo. Miles and Leo wrestled and played sports together. Leo died in a house fire, one of the first up-close images Miles had of death.

Although Miles grew up in a racially tolerant neighborhood, he well knew the meaning of prejudice. Just after the end of World War I, East St. Louis had been the site of some of the bloodiest race riots in U.S. history. With the postwar emigration of Southern blacks northward, white workers were suddenly faced with competition for low-paying, low-skill jobs. Some white workers lost their jobs when employers hired black laborers at lower pay. This economic threat, fueled by their intense dislike of blacks, caused groups of whites—usually poor, ignorant country people who had rarely encountered blacks—to rampage through East St. Louis for days on end, lynching and shooting black men, women, and children.

In some instances, white mobs had surrounded houses and factories, trapping those inside, and then setting the buildings afire. Those who made it out alive were shot down or hanged. The riots were finally quelled with the arrival of the National Guard. By then, 40 African Americans had been killed. Miles learned about the riots from old-timers in the neighborhood.

Another racial incident Miles remembered as a child was the time when, for no apparent reason, a white man in his forties chased him down a street, yelling "Nigger, nigger, nigger!" The terrified lad lost his pursuer and promptly made it to his father's office, whereupon the elder Davis, after hearing the story, got his shotgun and went in search of his son's tormentor. He didn't find him, but had he there is little doubt what he would have done.

Miles's childhood had its pleasant passages. He loved sports, especially football, baseball, and boxing. In baseball he was a fine fielding shortstop. And though small of stature and frame, a tenacious fighter like his idol, boxer Joe Louis. Miles also loved to swim and fish, activities that he and his brother, Vernon, enjoyed at their grandfather's farm in Arkansas where they spent the summers.

Miles's grandfather, Miles Dewey Davis, had been a very successful accountant and bookkeeper, mainly for the local white businessmen and farmers. He was so successful that he bought several hundred acres of land in rural Arkansas. This caused no end of envy and resentment in those types of whites who hated it if a black man succeeded. Every so often, local Ku Klux Klansmen would pay a little visit to Mr. Davis's farm, but he stood his ground. He was not about to be run off by rednecks in white sheets. One of his sons, Frank, acted as a bodyguard, and after a while the Davises had few problems with marauders.

In any case, country life was a paradise for Miles and Vernon. They rode horses, fished, swam, hiked, and frolicked with the farm's pigs, cows, and chickens. During walks with his grandfather or brother on lonely country back roads, Miles became aware of certain sounds: the hoot of an owl, the singing of crickets, and the occasional strains of blues or gospel being strummed, shouted, and wailed by black country folk. This sound, so solitary and haunting, so filled with emotion, never left him and influenced much of his later music. The opening bars on *Kind of Blue*, for example, were inspired by this childhood memory.

As carefree and fun as it was on the farm, Miles got in trouble now and then. He was, like so many boys, rather mischievous. One day he and his uncle William (who, oddly, was a year younger) busted up an entire watermelon patch, eating as many of them as they could. They thought they were really funny and laughed at their misdeed. Not surprisingly, they got sick. Miles's grandfather punished him by not letting Miles ride his horse for a week.

On the whole, Miles was indulged. His father, according to the great St. Louis horn player Clark Terry, "was the sort of guy who believed his son could do no wrong." That took quite a bit of belief because Miles did a lot that was wrong. One time he accidentally set fire to the garage, which could have burnt the house down. He often ruined brand new clothes when, on his way to church with his sister, he would see friends playing football or baseball and would join them.

His mother was the family disciplinarian. She would whip Miles or ask her husband to. On those occasions Doc Davis would take his son into a room, shut the door, pull off his belt, and ask his son to scream while he beat the bed or a chair. But as Miles put it in his autobiography, "He'd look at me all steely-eyed. I would have almost preferred his whipping me to the way he used to look right through me like I was nothing."

Miles was definitely his father's son. From him, Miles inherited his attitudes towards race, business, and everything else. An intelligent, proud man, Doc Davis was what was then called a "race man." He was an ardent supporter of the black nationalist Marcus Garvey, a pan-Africanist who was one of the founders of the "Back to Africa" movement. Doc Davis had disdain, if not downright contempt, for the National Association for the Advancement of Colored People (NAACP), which he saw as capitalist and pandering, filled with middle- and upper- middle-class black snobs. (Although decidedly middle-class himself, Doc Davis hated snobbery and self-hatred, and he did much charity work for his poorer patients, black and white.)

As for business, he told Miles to always count his money, a lesson that he himself had learned the hard way. Miles's grandfather had told Doc Davis the same thing as a boy and one day, as a test, gave him $1,000 to take to the bank. It was a hot day, and Doc Davis rode on a mule the 30 miles to the bank, only to discover that he was $50 short. So he rode back home the 30 miles, scared to death, through the blazing heat. When he got there and told his father that he had lost the money, Mr. Davis replied, "Did you count the money before you left? Do you know if it was all there?" Doc Davis had not, whereupon his father showed him the $50. "But didn't I tell you to count the money, anybody's money, even mine?" And Doc Davis had to go back to the bank, on the mule, in the blazing heat.

As an adult, Doc Davis enjoyed the finer things in life: good food, nice clothes, sleek, well-run cars. Miles himself later became legendary for the same, what with his tailored suits, Ferraris, and instinctive culinary talents.

Miles was also indulged—spoiled really—by his uncle Ferdinand. A Harvard man who had studied in Berlin, Ferdinand Davis was a bon vivant, a ladies' man, a wit, a scholar, and a fine writer and publisher (he founded the journal *Color*). Worldly, wise, full of high spirits, and blessed with good taste, Ferdinand left an indelible imprint on Miles, teaching him to be himself and to do things with style. Cleota Davis was none too pleased with Ferdinand spoiling Miles, with her husband already doing that. She was even less patient with Ferdinand's antics. Her feeling was that given Ferdinand's sophistication and bearing Miles would get airs and be ruined forever.

Early on music played an important, formative role in Miles's life. There was music in the streets, in the shops, on the radios; there was music everywhere. Miles spoke of first becoming attuned to music around the age of seven, listening to a morning radio show called *Harlem Rhythms*. He loved listening to this broadcast so much that he was often late for school.

On that show he first heard such jazz and blues giants as Louis Armstrong, Bessie Smith, Duke Ellington, Count Basie, Jimmie Lunceford, and Lionel Hampton. He would switch off the radio whenever a white-led band or a white musician came on, with the key exceptions of bandleader and trumpeter Harry James and the cornetist Bobby Hackett. (Years later, when Miles was at the forefront of bebop, Bobby Hackett, a foot soldier in the army of traditional jazz, surprised some by saying of Miles, "The other night I started to think I was sounding like Miles Davis, and I liked it.")

Around that time, Miles began taking private music lessons. In no time at all, music—and dressing sharp, like screen idols Cary Grant and Fred Astaire—occupied his mind to the exclusion of all else, even girls. There was little the Davis family could do to prevent this calamity. Cleota Davis did not much care for the idea of her son becoming a lazy, good-for-nothing, gin-house horn player. In her mind, that was a step down the social ladder. His father felt the same way, but he instinctively knew that music was to be his son's destiny. Doc Davis just hoped that Miles would not wind up playing in whorehouses and honky-tonks, that he would not disgrace the family name.

Now the problem was which instrument would Junior learn? Cleota Davis—who appeared to have an aversion to popular music, especially jazz and blues (though she did, when it was clear where her son was going, concede defeat and buy him two jazz disks, one by Duke Ellington and the other by Art Tatum, two strikingly excellent choices for someone who claimed to hate the music)—wanted her son to play the violin. But Miles argued with her. He wanted to learn trumpet so he could become like his idols Louis Armstrong and Harry James. In the end he got his way, and his father bought him a trumpet.

The next step was playing in the band at Crispus Attucks Middle School and, later, Lincoln High School. (The school would later be renamed Miles Dewey Davis High School.) His teacher and first mentor was Elwood Buchanan, a fine trumpeter more out of the Bix Beiderbecke school (lighter tone, understated) than out of Louis Armstrong's (hotter, fuller). Buchanan had nothing against Armstrong, perhaps the most important figure in the history of jazz, but the lighter, understated style of interpretation, which leaves more space for introspection and is in the middle register as opposed to the upper, suited Buchanan's temperament and abilities better.

According to Buchanan, when Miles arrived in his class, it was obvious to everyone that he had talent and a burning will to learn and improve. At first Miles was an expert mimic, particularly of Harry James, the famous, lushly romantic first trumpet in Benny Goodman's big band, who was renowned for his vibrato. There's nothing wrong with vibrato, but Miles was overdoing it a bit. One day, Buchanan stopped the band midway through a number and singled out Miles for correction.

"Look here, Miles," said Buchanan. "Don't come around here with that Harry James stuff, playing with all that vibrato. Stop shaking all those notes and trembling them, because you gonna be shaking enough when you get old." As much as Miles loved Harry James, it was good advice given at the right moment and an important first step towards developing his own voice.

Miles's other early mentor was a German émigré named Gustav, who was first trumpet in the St. Louis Symphony Orchestra. He taught Miles the old-fashioned way: practice, practice, practice. Miles later credited Gustav's harsh regimen, especially regarding the mastering of scales and other basics, with giving him the liberty to do other things, such as experiment and stretch. Discipline was key.

Gruff as Gustav was—he even called Miles his worst student, to his face—he had a soft spot for him. He told Dizzy Gillespie years later (who had come around to get one of Gustav's famous custom-made mouthpieces, something Miles did himself when he needed a new one) that Miles had always been his best and favorite student. But Miles had known that anyway, and he also had known that the old man was not going to let on what he really felt.

Miles's school band was filled with talent. Among the trumpeters (most of whom became famous, locally for the most part) were Levi Maddison, Shorty Baker, and Dewey Jackson. According to Miles, Maddison was a genius, an appraisal shared by those who heard him play. Miles even compared him to the great Dizzy Gillespie. Maddison, however, was mentally ill. He went around laughing to himself and would fall into deep depressions. Despite all these mood swings, he played like the Angel Gabriel. In Miles's words, "If he hadn't gone crazy and went to the nuthouse, people would have been talking about him today." In later years, whenever Miles was in St. Louis, he would visit Levi, chat with him, and ask him to hold his trumpet.

Slowly but surely, Miles began running with his band-mates, looking for places to play. One learns by doing, so for Miles playing in barrelhouses, honky-tonks, and sleazy clip joints was a continuation of his musical education. The St. Louis area, aside from being a rich breeding ground for musical talent, was an important venue for bands and combos doing cross-country tours. The region's residents were demanding and knowledgeable about music. Musicians couldn't slough off here and not expect to get razzed, or worse. Miles saw many of the same people he heard on the radio: the great Lester Young, Coleman Hawkins, bassist Jimmy Blanton, and, playing in Billy Eckstine's band, Charlie "Bird" Parker and Dizzy Gillespie. Miles even got to sit in once in a while, even with Bird and Diz. They told young Miles that if he was ever in New York to look them up.

Miles's tastes and knowledge were highly developed by this time. Given his nature, a mixture of his father's bluntness and temper and his mother's artistic sensibility and sensitivity, he would express in no uncertain terms what he thought of a bad show. In fact, he became something of a smart ass. For instance Miles and his good friend Bobby Danzig, a fine trumpeter in the school band with Miles, would go to a club and if, say, the drummer had set up his kit ineptly or the trumpeter missed a note or could not play all that well, they would loudly display their contempt.

When Miles was about thirteen, yet another seminal figure entered his life: the gifted trumpeter and flügelhornist Clark Terry. Their first meeting was in Carbondale, Illinois, where Miles and his schoolmates were playing. Upon hearing that a fellow trumpeter from East St. Louis was playing at a nearby beer garden, Miles and company, still in their uniforms, decided to check him out. Clark Terry was then regarded as the hottest thing around St. Louis. (Terry eventually wound up playing for Duke Ellington for nine years and later formed his own successful big bands and small combos.) During a break in the set, Miles boldly went up and began asking Terry all sorts of technical questions: How did you phrase this? How did you hold your horn? How do you breathe? Terry, more interested in his pretty female fans, brusquely told Miles to blow.

Miles was hurt but quickly recovered. He swore to himself that not only would he surpass Terry as a trumpet player but he would outdress and out-hip him as well. Terry's snub seemed to inspire Miles. He went to more jam sessions and now and then even sat in with some of the big boys coming through town. These experiences boosted his self-confidence and fueled his growing desire to be a professional musician—an ambition that his mother detested and did all she could to discourage. They argued frequently and heatedly about his future, but Miles was adamant. Mrs. Davis finally relented.

Irene Birth also had something to do with this change in the climate. Miles had blocked out everything, even girls, because of his music. But soon he began paying attention to the opposite sex. Though he dated infrequently, he did manage to see Irene enough that they became an item. Doc Davis was disappointed in Miles's choice for a serious girlfriend, probably because Irene was poor and uneducated. Cleota Davis, though, saw Irene as an anchor in her son's life as wayward musician.

Although still in high school, Miles played in pick-up bands, earning money. Despite a demanding schedule, his schoolwork did not suffer. Indeed, Miles sailed through his classes. At one point he considered medicine as a possible career. Altruism—selfless regard for the welfare of others— spurred his interest in becoming a doctor. He was spending a lot of time at Irene's home, in a rather run-down, squalid area of town. Miles was close to her family. The youngest brother, William, of whom he was especially fond, got very sick, probably with influenza. The only doctor who would venture into a nasty slum to treat a poor black child took one look at William and told the family there was no hope.

Miles went back to his father and asked how anyone could be so cold-blooded. Doc Davis told Miles the facts of life then and there: money talks, people walk. For a brief time, Miles changed his intended career to medicine. But, try as he might, and as good as his aims were, the lure of the musical spotlight was too strong.

When he was 15, Miles got the break that forever sealed his fate to be a musician and that would keep him from ever leading the conventional middle-class life of his parents: he got a job in a band. It was simple really. Miles was going on about the hottest band in town, Eddie Randle's Blue Devils, to Irene, when she dared him to audition for them. Not being one to back down from a dare, Miles picked up the gauntlet, auditioned, and was hired on the spot.

Now Miles was making good money, $50 a week, working part-time, and because he was in such a burning bright band, his playing took off as never before. He acquired a reputation for playing fast, mean, and lean.

Clark Terry heard about this hot, new trumpeter, and

In 1944, Miles (back row, far right) plays trumpet in
Eddie Randle's orchestra in St. Louis. It was
the 17-year-old trumpeter's first professional job.

one night went over to check him out. He was astounded by what he heard. It also dawned on him, as the evening wore on, that the little fellow in the sharp, clean clothes looked familiar. He could not quite place the face. Then Terry realized he was the kid he'd sussed months back.

After the set Miles came over and reintroduced himself as the kid "you wouldn't even talk to over in Carbondale." Terry laughed, apologized, and thereafter he and Miles became the very closest of friends, running together to all the clubs, sitting in and jamming all hours of the night. Later that year, however, Terry left the scene.

On December 7, 1941, the Japanese bombed Pearl Harbor, bringing the United States into World War II. Young men, scarcely boys, flocked to join the armed forces. Clark Terry, six years Miles's senior, was no exception. He joined the army and was sent up to play in the elite army band in Michigan. Ernie Royal, Willie Smith, and a lot of players from the bands of Lionel Hampton and Jimmie Lunceford, were already up there. Miles, without Terry's camaraderie and example, grew despondent and even considered joining himself. He had too many other distractions, though: Irene, his family, finishing school, and his music. He was too young to join the armed services, anyway.

In 1943, Irene announced that she was pregnant. She liked to run around, so Miles might not have been the father of Irene's daughter, Cheryl. Miles may have married Irene Birth around this time (the circumstances are unclear). Most certainly he was father to Irene's second child, a son named Gregory.

In terms of family, Miles's relationship with his father was, as it had always been, excellent. His relationship with his mother, however, worsened to the point where they were barely on speaking terms. This was also the state of affairs between Doc Davis and his wife. After years of mis-

where the bebop revolution was in full swing. He roamed 52nd Street ("the Street," for short), where the more polished music found its way to such clubs as Three Deuces, Onyx Club, Kelly's Stable, and the Spotlite.

Ideally located right smack in the center of town, not far from the military stations of midtown and the naval stations of the West Side, 52nd Street between Fifth and Sixth Avenues teemed with clubs. In addition to the fun-loving servicemen chasing wine, women, and song, some members of the local gentry, so-called café-society types like journalists, actors, wayward aristocrats, bohemians, and preppies, liked to jitterbug as well—some of them even went up to Minton's.

Miles had no luck tracking down Bird or Diz for the first few weeks, but in the meantime he heard a lot of great music: Lester Young ("the President" or "Prez," for short), Billie Holiday, Sonny Stitt, Fats Navarro, Freddie Webster, Howard McGhee, Bud Powell, Thelonious Monk, Sarah Vaughan, and many others.

Miles finally did run into Dizzy Gillespie in the street. To his delight, Diz remembered him as the talented young trumpeter from back in St. Louis. Unfortunately, Diz, too, had not seen Bird, not in weeks, and they were supposed to be gigging together. It dawned on Miles that Bird was perhaps a bit unreliable.

This meeting began a close, lifelong friendship between Miles and Diz. Miles idolized Diz, and at the time Diz's rapid-fire, high-octane style influenced Miles's playing (indeed it influenced everybody's). But more importantly, Diz took the young musician under his wing, showed him around New York, introduced him to all the musicians and club owners, taught him a few things on the horn, invited him over to meet his wife and have supper, and generally looked out for Miles. Diz kept him laughing and in good

Dizzy Gillespie strikes a humorous pose for this 1944
photograph. Diz, a titan of bebop, was Miles's mentor
and one of his dearest friends.

spirits. As Miles himself put it, "As much as I loved Bird back then, if it hadn't been for Dizzy I wouldn't be where I am today."

Another giant Miles met during his Bird hunt was the tenor saxophonist Coleman Hawkins, or "Bean," as his peers called him. Like Miles, Bean was from the Midwest, Kansas City to be exact (which was also Bird's hometown). Miles told Bean about his search for Bird, and Bean laughed in an elder statesman way and solemnly advised Miles to forget Bird—he was a genius but an unreliable parasite. Bean advised Miles to stick to getting his degree at Juilliard.

This was not what Miles wanted to hear. He had a quick temper and was cocky. Even though it was Coleman Hawkins talking, Miles ripped into him, telling him he did not need lectures, he was receiving them aplenty at Juilliard. He then stomped off to find Bird.

Touched by Miles's spunk and sensitivity, Bean befriended the brooding young upstart, introducing him to many of the musicians mentioned and even engaging him for a few gigs when his regular trumpet could not make it. Working with Bean was yet another great learning experience, a chance to work with a jazz legend and a man who helped transform the role of the tenor saxophone in jazz. Bean's big, fat, ballad-rich sound came straight out of Louis Armstrong's style of trumpet playing, a natural enough progression, though still derivative.

At the time, Bean was one of the few nontrumpeters in jazz, aside from singers, to achieve any real fame or recognition. Lester Young, a true original, had been the first real innovator on the tenor sax, with his own unique sound, which was lighter, faster, ballad rich. Early on he evinced Hawkinslike power in his playing, but he preferred to be sweet or suggestive where Bean would be ferocious or aggressive. Prez was also a brilliant improviser, one of the greatest ever. With Bean and Prez, and, later, Bird (who played alto to distinguish himself from Bean and Prez), the saxophone gradually replaced the trumpet as the lead instrument in jazz.

In any case, the Miles and Bean combination was a good one, with Bean's milewide, riffing style contrasting nicely with his younger charge's well-tempered, well-spaced, middle-register flourishes that darted in and out, creating space and settings.

Miles finally caught up with Bird one cool fall night at the Heatwave, a famous Harlem nightspot. Miles was listening to the house band tear up the place when suddenly Bird surprised him on his way out. As usual, Bird looked like hell, and the first words out of his mouth, in his mock English accent, were, "Hey, Miles, I heard you been looking for me." He invited Miles back to the cozy confines of the club.

They walked in together, Miles helping Bird along; Bird was stoned and had his arm around Miles. Inside Bird was greeted as if he were a king, everyone bowing and scraping, getting him drinks, seeing that he was comfortable. Miles, by association, was also deferred to as one of the king's lieges. But before they sat down to chew the fat, Bird took the stage, picked up a sax, and proceeded to blow away the other musicians—heroin, whiskey, stimulants, or whatever he was hopped up on not withstanding. According to Miles:

Bird changed the minute he put his horn in his mouth. Shit, he went from looking real down and out to having all this power and beauty just bursting out of him. It was amazing the transformation that took place once he started playing. He was twenty-four at the time, but when he wasn't playing he looked older, especially off stage. But his whole appearance changed as soon as he put that horn in his mouth. He could play like a motherfucker even when he was almost falling-down drunk and nodding off behind heroin. Bird was something else.

Miles had found his god. He was overwhelmed when Bird actually remembered when and where they first met. They spent the rest of the night talking about music, life, and women. Miles brought Bird home to crash at his rooming house apartment, located at 147th Street and Broadway. By this time, Irene Birth and her baby had shown up at Miles's doorstep and were living with him. Bird stayed on as the household's other little bundle of joy, the 250-pound son they both wanted so much.

Bird settled into Miles and Irene's little love nest and acted as if the tiny, cramped Harlem apartment was his own. Bird would ask Miles for money, and Miles, who received an adequate allowance from his family back home, would lend him some. Miles never saw any of the money back.

And when Miles refused to hand over some cash, Bird wouldn't hesitate to take Miles's horn, cuff links, or anything else of value to a pawnshop to get the money he needed for drugs. Bird even borrowed clothes. Sometimes after coming off a binge, he would show up at the Davis residence missing his jacket or shirt. So when it was time for a gig and Bird needed a nice suit, Miles's clothes would have to do. Miles was not too happy to get back his snazzy Brooks Brothers suits all misshapen or ripped, but what else could he do? Bird was a genius.

Bird also had the nice, nasty habit of shooting up heroin at Miles's apartment. If it wasn't heroin, he would smoke marijuana or drink liquor till he dropped. All this came as a shock to Miles. Although he was a father at a rather tender age, he didn't drink or do drugs.

Legendary saxophonist Charlie "Bird" Parker opened Miles's eyes to the infinite potential of jazz as an art form.

Bird would also have women over. There were many. After a while it came as no surprise to come home and find Bird having sex with some woman on the living room or kitchen floor. Much more unpleasant were other visitors—menacing dope pushers and gangsters who were either delivering drugs or showing up demanding payment. On those occasions when Bird was broke, he would sometimes point at Miles and say, "Oh, he'll take care of it." To avoid the risk of a beating or worse, Miles would fork over the cash.

Bird would sometimes disappear for days or weeks on end, and the dope dealers would come around, scaring the living daylights out of Irene and the baby. It was probably this more than anything else that prompted Miles to ask Bird kindly to leave the premises.

Despite the constant troubles with Bird, Miles began spending more and more time at the University of Bebop under the tutelage of professors Bird and Diz. Although Bird was his idol, Miles's master was Dizzy, the clown prince of bebop. Diz showed Miles how to play certain passages in difficult tunes, such as Thelonious Monk's "'Round Midnight" or Bird's own "Koko" or "Cherokee." And, most important of all, Diz encouraged Miles to nurture his own talent, to find his own voice. Diz also taught Miles how to play piano, which was instrumental in helping Miles realize his ambitions in composing and arranging.

Dizzy was also Miles's best teacher because as a trumpeter he understood the physical demands of playing the instrument. One thing that Miles had difficulty in doing, for instance, was matching Diz high note for high note. Technically it seemed this was beyond his capacity. Miles asked professor Diz why he could not play high like him. "Because you don't hear up there," he replied.

As a result Miles, with Diz's almost fatherly advice and help (though he was only nine years older than Miles), concentrated on his strong point, the middle register. Miles rounded out his sound, cut his notes, implying themes and ideas rather than asserting them, following a set pattern, or going full blast. (Miles could be beautifully and heart-breakingly bold when he wanted to be; listen to "Bye Bye Blackbird," "Someday My Prince Will Come," or "Stella by Starlight.") Miles had a richer, warmer tone than Diz, and even though he didn't "hear" or play as fast and as furiously as Bird and Diz, when the occasion warranted it he could bring it to the plate. Listen to any live recording of "Walkin'," and you'll hear it.

Miles was rather dramatic in his playing. He had the timing and sense of a great actor like Orson Welles, who influenced Miles with his way of speaking lines. With his understatement setting up the occasional stirring note or deeply felt passage, Miles forces the listener to really listen; it's impossible to be indifferent when Miles is playing.

Often when Miles was with Bird and Diz, he would just sit back, his tongue almost hanging out, taking it all in—those faster than fast blistering, scorching solos that Bird and Diz did so well. And then the dauntless youth would be prodded up to the mike. The young player would give it his best shot, and although Bird and Diz nodded their approval (they really did approve), Miles always felt he was not keeping up. He was easily discouraged, especially when audiences would tune him out after getting their fill of the main attractions.

Miles had never lacked confidence before, but now he found himself sitting out, even calling it an early night at times. Miles asked at one point, "What do you guys need me for?" Bird kindly encouraged him, "Don't be afraid. Just go up and play." So while Bird may have been a "greedy motherfucker," as Miles sometimes called him, he could be just as generous in his encouragement and advice.

It was not long before Miles began to grow restless at Juilliard. After doing all-nighters with the likes of Bird, Diz,

Bean, Max Roach, Bud Powell, Monk, Fats Navarro, Freddie Webster, Eddie "Lockjaw" Davis, Sonny Stitt, J. J. Johnson, Tadd Dameron, Kenny "Klook" Clarke and then doing a daily grind at Juilliard, playing "two notes every ninety bars," Miles would be exhausted and frustrated. Classes bored him to tears, and American music—much less jazz, blues, or gospel—was rarely mentioned. In one of his classes, Miles gave one old blue-haired woman a hard time about never having heard of Duke Ellington or even Scott Joplin.

Miles had to walk. With the exceptions of one or two professors and teachers who were hip to the Street and the uptown scene, there was hardly anything or anyone of any relevance for Miles at Juilliard. He literally could not stand the place. He guessed that the kind of instruction he was receiving there would not matter to him anyway. He did not much care for classical music (he had a particular bias against Beethoven), except for twentieth century composers (he loved the work of Stravinsky, Berg, and Prokofiev). Miles also knew that no matter how much he practiced, no matter how well he played, no matter how many pieces in the repertoire he mastered, no symphony orchestra at the time was going to hire him because of his race.

One day Miles decided to quit, just like that. A semester and a half was enough. The first person he told about this was his good friend, the trumpeter Freddie Webster (a major influence on Miles, particularly in his ballad playing). In Miles's own words, he couldn't just "call up my old man and say, 'Listen, Dad, I'm working with some cats named Bird and Diz, so I'm gonna quit school.'" So Miles took that long, lonesome train ride out to St. Louis, walked into Doc Davis's office, ignored the Do Not Disturb sign, and laid it out to him.

"Listen, Dad," Miles told his father. "There is something happening in New York. The music is changing, the styles, and I want to be in it, with Bird and Diz. So I came back to tell you that I'm quitting Juilliard because what they're teaching me is white and I'm not interested in that."

Doc Davis okayed Miles's plan. As parting advice, Doc Davis pointed to a mockingbird right outside his office window and told his son, "Miles, you hear that bird outside the window. He's a mockingbird. He don't have a sound of his own. He copies everybody's sound, and you don't want to do that. You want to be your own man, have your own sound. That's what it's really about."

4 Miles in Stride

The actual hiring of Miles Davis by Charlie Parker was a simple matter. One day Dizzy Gillespie quit the band, just like that. He had had enough of Bird's drug taking, his drinking and wenching, his beating him out of his money, and various other high jinks. Dizzy may have been an eccentric, but he was a professional and expected to be treated that way.

Not long after this, Bird and Miles were in a club together when the club owner came up and asked, "So, Bird, who's going to be your new trumpet player?" Bird turned to Miles, tapped him lightly on the shoulder as if he were knighting him, and declared, "Here's my trumpet player right here, Miles Davis."

After the hot sound of Dizzy Gillespie, Miles's leaner, more linear style of playing was just what Bird needed to underline his own, to set him off. Bird and Diz were very close in style. They were hard boppers, constantly improvising, fast, with lots of notes. Dizzy, especially, emphasized higher and higher notes and scales of the upper register.

*Miles plays with the Charlie Parker combo in
1947. After dropping out of Juilliard, Miles
succeeded Dizzy Gillespie as the trumpeter in
Parker's band.*

Miles had a more balanced, middle-register tone. In contrast to Dizzy, Miles was not an attacker but rather a shaper of notes or passages, a path setter. He would cut in, dart in and out of Bird's playing, be the setting to Bird's jewel. (John Coltrane served in this same role for Miles years later.) Bird was hot. Miles was cool. The contrast in styles and intonations caught on after some initial doubt on the part of Dizzy aficionados. Some bebop purists were horrified with the switch. To them, Dizzy was the other high priest of bebop; this Johnny-come-lately Davis was profaning the temple with his uncluttered solos. But it soon became apparent to these critics that Miles gave Bird more room to be Bird.

Soon, though, Miles had developed his own following and, more important, his own sound. One of the traits that distinguished Miles's playing was that instead of playing against or in tandem with the lead horn (in this case Bird) or the occasional singer like Annie Ross or Sarah Vaughan, Miles left a lot of space for the lead, playing a little before or a little after it, never over it.

Again, some of the bebop purists misinterpreted Miles's grace as a form of musical cowardice. Why was he not dueling with the lead? Why wasn't he trying to cut the other guy to shreds? Miles was certainly capable of this, but to him music was about cooperation, not competition. It was about ensemble work, not a bunch of individuals vying for the brass ring. Miles loved to jam as much as the next guy, but when he did, it was in the spirit of friendship. Over and over again, in everything he said and did, Miles emphasized this team-player aspect of his personality.

In interview after interview and in his autobiography, Miles always accentuated the positive when it came to his fellow musicians—how much he respected and loved his peers, such as Bird, Diz, Bean, Bud Powell, Charles Mingus,

Monk, Clark Terry, Max Roach, and others. Miles, however, wasn't coy about giving objective, often blunt, assessments of their shortcomings.

Miles was thrilled to be playing with Bird, but joining forces with the unreliable Parker entailed burdens Miles never even dreamt of. What Miles and others couldn't fathom was why Bird had to be the way he was. "Bird knew better," Miles once reflected. "He was an intellectual. He used to read novels, poetry, history, stuff like that. He could hold a conversation with almost anybody on all kinds of things." But then, as Miles put it, "He was a genius and most geniuses are greedy."

Worst of all, Bird took advantage of Miles's admiration and love for him as a musician, something Bird did to a great many people in order to get money to buy heroin or to cop a place to stay or a free drink. Genius, of course, draws admiration and, thereby, admirers, some of whom will put up with almost anything to be close to the flame.

Well, Bird burnt them all, and such was the case with Miles when Bird began telling the nastier pushers that "Jim (his name for Miles, a nickname popular among musicians at that time) here will take care of you." It got so bad with the dealers busting in demanding money that Irene returned briefly to East St. Louis. Miles finally put his foot down; by then Bird had found a new nest downtown.

In between gigs with Bird, Miles played with Coleman Hawkins, Illinois Jacquet, and Eddie "Lockjaw" Davis. Through playing with Hawkins, Miles came to know Thelonious Monk, who played piano in the band. Monk was unforgettable. Large and powerful, bearlike even, Monk was an offbeat character who, despite his well-cut suits, favored odd hats and headgear—anything from an old, beat-up top hat to an Indian headdress—which sent the whole ensemble askew.

Monk's appearance belied his manner, though. Like John Coltrane, Monk was a strong, silent type. He was far away in his thoughts and often cryptic when he spoke. Unlike Coltrane, Monk was not a gentle soul, not all peace and love. Instead, he was ruminative and moody.

As a pianist Monk was anything but traditional. Although he had a bit of the stride piano of Count Basie, Fats Waller, and Willie "the Lion" Smith in him, his style of play was more disjointed, more off, or "wrong." Some critics asserted that Monk could not play piano correctly and that his "style" was a cover. In a legendary anecdote, Art Tatum, perhaps the greatest virtuoso of jazz piano and one of the greatest pianists of the twentieth century, purportedly had the gall to tell Monk to his face that he couldn't play. Monk, his pride wounded, asked Tatum to name any tune he could think of and he would play it straight through, as written, which he proceeded to do. After that Art Tatum never again doubted Monk's musicianship.

Miles Davis immediately recognized Monk for the genius he was, not only as a pianist but also as an innovator and highly original composer. A favorite story of Miles's was about the time he was learning to play "'Round Midnight," Monk's most famous composition. They were working in Bean's band and every night, after Miles finished playing it, he would ask Monk if he had played it right. Monk would look at him gravely and say, "You didn't play it right." This went on for some time. Other times Monk would feign exasperation, put a demonic look on his face, and tell Miles, "No, that's not the way to play it." Finally, after a few months, after Miles had asked for the umpteenth time Monk replied, "Yeah, that's the way you play it." As Miles put it, "Man, that made me happier than a motherfucker, happier than a pig

Thelonious Monk relaxes in a nightclub dressing room. The offbeat, moody pianist was one of the leaders of the bebop movement.

in shit! I'd gotten the sound down." " 'Round Midnight" later became one of Miles's biggest hits on an album of the same name.

Another Miles and Monk anecdote was about the time they did a session together recording "Bag's Groove." Because of Monk's unusual manner of playing and his propensity to lead and dictate the direction the music took regardless of who was there or what was being played, Miles asked Monk to lay out while he was soloing. It was not that he disliked Monk's playing; it was just that Miles did not want him playing over his solo.

According to legend, Miles and Monk nearly came to blows, but Miles insisted that the story was blown out of all proportion. There was no violence, not even any real raising of voices. Besides, Miles thought it would have been madness to tangle with anyone the size of Monk: "He could have just squashed me if he wanted to."

In Bird's band, Miles was closest to the drummer, Max Roach. They often roomed together and were like brothers. Indeed, among bebop circles Miles and Max were gaining reputations for being the next real things. One attitude they certainly shared, one not shared by many of their predecessors, was that they were just musicians, nothing else. Miles and Max resolved that they were not going to smile or entertain or introduce songs or do a little song and dance or tap dance or any kind of Uncle Tomming. Like it or leave it, let the music speak for itself. Bud Powell, Mingus, and Monk also felt this way.

Perhaps such an attitude was in the air at the time among all kinds of artists. The postwar era in America saw the advent of such cultural phenomena as the abstract expressionist movement, or New York school, in art, which featured somber, serious abstract art, heroic gestures, and lots of dripping paint on enormous canvases, and the rise in theater of such serious playwrights as Tennessee Williams, William Inge, and Arthur Miller.

In literature the Beats, a motley crew who rejected middle-class life and values, were all the rage. The work of such writers as Jack Kerouac, Allen Ginsburg, William Burroughs, Gregory Corso, Gary Snyder, and Lawrence Ferlinghetti shocked the literary establishment and attracted much publicity and many imitators. African-American writers, too, were coming to the fore, with Richard Wright and James Baldwin emerging from the huge shadow cast by the Harlem Renaissance poet Langston Hughes. This angry-young-man attitude filled the air and perhaps found its way into bebop. After all, jazz musicians, no less than writers or actors or directors, are not islands unto themselves.

Thus far, bebop had been an East Coast thing. Then in late 1946, after the Street had been closed down by one of the New York City Police Department's periodic vice raids—in truth, Midtown residents didn't like so many black musicians and fans frequenting the neighborhood—Diz's agent, Billy Shaw, convinced a Los Angeles nightclub owner that bebop was what they needed out West to spice up their nights. The club owner wanted Bird; Diz did not want Bird going out, but in the end he gave in. Al Haig, Milt Jackson, Stan Levey, and Ray Brown filled out the band.

Miles, with little to do in New York, made a brief visit to East St. Louis with Irene. There, the great alto and bandleader Benny Carter happened to be in town performing. He was en route to the West Coast, and he asked Miles to jump on board. In Los Angeles Miles played with Benny's band in the evenings and did matinees; after hours he hooked up with Bird for a little club jamming. The music with Bird and Diz and company was so hot and sizzling that Bird was able to get a recording contract with Dial Records. Miles was asked to sit in, which he happily did.

Playing night after night with Bird and participating in a recording session made Miles feel 10 feet tall. His music with Bird and Diz was sizzling hot, but his gig with Benny Carter's Orchestra was decidedly not. It was not so much Benny's fault, who was and still is a great musician, but it was the old, tired arrangements the band was using—slow dance music and some swing played to a totally unhip, older crowd. Miles left Benny Carter, but there were no hard feelings on either side.

Through Bird and Diz, Miles met the innovative bassist and composer Charles Mingus. Born in L.A. and a player about town, Mingus did not miss a night at the Finale, the club where the bebop rebels were tearing it up. A tall, powerful, imposing man, Mingus was very opinionated and effusive, and a bit of a dandy in his manner of dress. He became a very good friend of Bird's, admired and loved him, and a firm friend of Miles's as well. He was so talented, arguably one of the two or three greatest bassists in jazz, that everyone knew it was only a matter of time before he made the big move to New York, where everything was happening. From Mingus, Miles learned new ways to hear music, inverting chords, playing a composition in a key other than the one it was written for. Like Monk, Mingus expanded Miles's field of vision, opened up his ears a bit more, shook up his preconceptions.

When it came time to do the sessions, it looked at first as if Bird was not going to make it. Uncertain of himself, unable to obtain a steady supply of heroin, Bird was drinking everything in sight, reeling around drunk in public, looking a hellish mess. In New York, Bird was God, but to the L.A. and Hollywood crowds, this shabby, plastered black man was less than zero.

That all changed when Bird got in the studio. Normally unreliable, Bird showed up for the session. He, Diz,

Charles Mingus posed for this late 1940s
publicity shot. Miles first met the ace bassist
in Los Angeles in 1946.

Miles, Lucky Thompson on tenor sax, Arv Garrison on guitar, Vic McMillan on bass, Roy Parker on drums, and Dodo Mamarosa on piano, recorded such classics as "Night in Tunisia," "Yardbird Suite," and "Ornithology."

Despite the success of the sessions and the club dates, Bird was physically and mentally breaking down. He still played dates, usually brilliantly, still looked a wreck, but time, at least on the West Coast, was running out for him. One drunken night Bird accidentally set fire to himself in bed (he had passed out with a cigarette in his fingers), nearly killing himself. After somehow putting out the fire, Bird ran out into the street, buck naked, and wandered about in confusion. The police picked him up. Soon thereafter, he was committed to the state mental hospital in Camarillo, where he was given shock treatments.

Work in L.A. dried up for Miles until Billy Eckstine came along. Impressed with how Miles had developed since he had last heard him, Mr. B hired him on the spot for a West Coast tour. Admiring Miles's skills, he secretly paid him a much higher salary than the other trumpeters in the band. At the time, Eckstine's band was the hottest one in the land, and B was a singer whose popularity at its peak rivaled that of such singers as Nat "King" Cole and Frank Sinatra. The Billy Eckstine Band got the best gigs, played the best clubs, attracted the hippest audiences.

Miles really dug the scene, and it was with B's band that he began to dabble with hard drugs. At this point Miles was still something of an aw-shucks rube underneath his hard-ass bebop attitude. He rarely smoked anything racier than a cigarette or drank anything stronger than a beer. Robert Dotson, the trumpet player who sat next to him, introduced Miles's nasal passages to cocaine. And Gene Ammons, a great tenor, gave Miles his first ride on heroin, snorting all the way. At first Miles did not much care for coke or smack—hardly anyone does the first time—but he noted how relaxed he was after indulging, especially the heroin. Yes, maybe there was something in this brown sugar after all. Look at Bird. (Yeah, look at Bird, still in the nuthouse.)

Another bad lesson Miles learned in B's band—from B himself—was how to handle women: treat them like dogs, and they would come running; beat them and slap them around if they got their noses out of joint. B also had a unique way of getting rid of bores, journalists, and people on the make—he'd just tell them to get out of his face. Simple as that. Short and sweet. B was an excellent teacher, and Miles was a brilliant pupil.

By the time L.A. became a drag, the Street had reopened, and it was time to return to New York. Miles went back without Bird, who was still institutionalized. Finally though, Bird was released, a new man, not drinking so much anymore but still using heroin. Upon his return the band reunited, and they were off ripping up all the clubs on 52nd Street and uptown.

The weak links in the band were, according to Miles and Max, on bass and piano. Bassist Tommy Potter choked the bass as if he hated it, prompting Miles to say, "Tommy, let that woman loose!" In truth, despite his lack of flair, Potter kept good time. Pianist Duke Jordan, however, just took up space. Miles and Max's first choice for a pianist was Bud Powell. The problem was that Bud did not have much use for Bird. They played together many times—most memorable would be the legendary Massie Hall concert in Toronto in 1953, regarded by some as the greatest jazz concert of all time—but Bud was reluctant to be around Bird for any length of time. This disdain and wariness seemed rather one-sided. Bird would have loved nothing better than to have Bud around, and they had things in common. Both were geniuses. Both were junkies.

Bud was also just a bit mentally unstable. After getting beaten up by a bouncer at the Savoy, he began shooting up as if there were no tomorrow and drinking to the point of blindness. Bud began having fits and seizures and would not speak to anyone for weeks on end. He would sit around and stare in a seemingly catatonic state. Eventually his mother had him institutionalized, where he too was given shock treatments. He was never the same after that, not as a man or a musician.

It was most likely differences in temperaments that kept these two from uniting in the same band. Bird was a joker, a clown, whereas Bud was very serious and quiet.

In any case the one time Miles got his wish was on a Dial record called *The Charlie Parker All Stars*, which was notable for other reasons as well. For one thing Miles received his first composer credit on an album for a tune called "Donna Lee." The other significant event was that a young arranger named Gil Evans heard "Donna Lee" and came around to see Bird about arranging it for the Claude Thornhill Orchestra. Bird referred the gawky Canadian to Miles, and in no time they were having a long discussion about music and arrangements of other tunes. They saw eye to eye almost instantly, Miles saying later that Gil "was the only one who could pick up on what I was thinking musically." They also hit it off instantly and became lifelong close friends. Gil Evans was also—very notable—probably Miles's first adult white friend, which to an extent lessened his view that all whites were racist devils. Gil Evans and Miles Davis were to make beautiful music together.

As things turned out, this time round with Bird was not any better than the previous times. Bird getting high was a given, but now he was nodding off on stage, playing his solos attentively but not playing behind or with the sidemen. And, again, to feed the monster Bird was cheating his

Gil Evans relaxes in his home. Miles collaborated with
Evans on many of Davis's classic recordings, including
Birth of the Cool and Sketches of Spain.

colleagues out of the money due them. Miles got fed up. At one point during a torrid argument, when he had been told there was no more money for the band, he threatened to cut up Bird with a broken bottle. Bird produced the bucks. Sometimes, it took drastic action to get the great man's attention.

Around this turbulent time, when Miles was not playing with Bird's band, he began working with Gil Evans on a different kind of music, which came to be known as cool jazz. Cool is in direct contrast with bebop. It is slower in tempo, and the solo voices are more carefully delineated and more clearly heard. The sound, the doubling up on chords, and the voicelike aspect of the instrumentation is, Miles asserted in his autobiography, black in origin, not white (as if that really mattered). He argued that it came from the music of Duke Ellington and his great composer/arranger Billy Strayhorn, and bandleader/arranger Fletcher Henderson. Other influences were undoubtedly Lester Young and Bix Beiderbecke.

Miles was quick to point this out because much to his dismay (and perhaps overactive imagination) white critics and fans were all too quick to champion the new, cool school. Bebop was too fast, too difficult, too raw and unrestrained, too sweaty—too black. A simplification, perhaps, but there may be something in this.

When Miles turned to cool, he caught hell because he was working with too many white musicians and not enough blacks. In addition to Gil, who was the principal arranger and not an instrumentalist, there was baritone saxophonist/arranger Gerry Mulligan. There was also the pianist Al Haig, who had played with Miles before on the West Coast tour with Bird (the great black pianist John Lewis would sometimes sit in for Haig). But the wonderful alto sax player Lee Konitz drew the most ire; Konitz had been picked over the great tenor man Sonny Stitt, and some observers questioned why Miles had selected Konitz over "one of his own." Miles at first wanted Stitt, but after several rehearsals he decided that Konitz's sound and tone was better suited to the ensemble as a whole. Stitt was a bolder, more dynamic player, the last of the great all-night jammers; Konitz had a more lyrical, lighter touch. Miles's choice was not a statement on race or who was the better musician; it was about whose sound would blend in best for the project at hand. As Miles put it, "If a guy could play as good as Lee Konitz played—and that's who they were most mad about, because there were a lot of black alto players around—I would hire him every time, and wouldn't give a damn if he was green with red breath. I'm hiring a motherfucker to play, not for what color he is."

In short order the nonet found a home at the Roost for two weeks and shortly thereafter, with a slightly different lineup, *Birth of the Cool* (1949) was cut. This seminal recording launched the cool movement in jazz and continues to influence musicians to this day. The collaboration between Miles and Gil sealed their personal and professional relationship, one that was based on mutual admiration and respect.

Another nice thing that happened at this time came as a complete surprise: Miles's childhood idol, Duke Ellington, decided that he needed Miles Davis in his band. A gofer brought Miles around to the old Brill Building on Broadway and 49th where the Duke had his office. Miles had died and gone to heaven as far as he was concerned. He was dressed sharper than ever. He had to be: he was meeting the man who was the definition of finesse itself. So, imagine his surprise when, upon entering the Duke's inner sanctum, he sees the Duke in his shorts holding a little scantily clad lovely in his lap. Miles was taken aback some, but the Duke got right down to business. He told Miles how much he liked his playing and his style and proposed that Miles join his band in the fall.

With great regret Miles turned down the offer, but not until he had told the Duke how much he and his music meant to him and how flattered he was to even be considered for a job in the greatest band of them all. Then they talked a little about *Birth of the Cool* and a few other things and parted on good terms. Miles never ceased to wonder what might have happened had he said yes, but as he told a friend, after playing with Mr. B he could not go back to being in a big band ever again. Miles was already a jump ahead.

Shortly after this, Miles left Bird. He was taken seriously as an artist and musician now and had his own following. His attitude had changed, and Bird's increasing lack of professionalism was getting on his nerves. It was not enough that Bird beat him and the others out of their money or that he was always late for gigs or nodding out on stage, but now Bird was becoming a comedian. Such on-stage stunts as shooting a cap gun at Al Haig or Tommy Potter, letting the air out of a balloon in front of the microphone, and generally playing the fool were too much. Miles walked off the stage one night after he finished soloing. Max Roach quit that night as well.

Miles played around in different bands, but a real change in his life and music was just around the corner. Tadd Dameron, the great pianist, arranger, and composer, asked Miles to join his band as a replacement for Fats Navarro who was in steadily declining health due to heroin addiction (Navarro, a great bebop original and standard-bearer, died in 1950, a shell of his former greatness). It was a nice change to be with Dameron, a nontemperamental, easygoing sort.

Dameron took the band to Paris in early 1949. The band consisted of Dameron on piano, Miles on trumpet, James Moody on tenor, Kenny "Klook" Clarke on drums, and a French bassist named Pierre Michelot. Paris was a revelation for Miles, as it has been for so many artists and writers. It was his first trip outside the United States, and in Paris, Miles was treated like royalty. The food was better, the women were chic, the air was soft, the coffee was rich and delicious. The city cast its inextricable spell on him, and Miles fell in love with the place.

Miles even met some of the locals, including Pablo Picasso and Jean-Paul Sartre. The band was a hit, receiving ovation after ovation, flowers, and invitations to play other clubs. They were also an enormous hit at the Paris Jazz Festival, where they jammed with legendary American expatriate jazzman Sidney Bechet, who has a street named after him in Paris. The only time Miles had ever felt so good in his life was when he first heard Bird and Diz in B's band and when he was playing in Diz's big band. Indeed, Miles felt so good and relaxed that he even took to calling out the tunes in French. (As a rule, he never announced anything.)

And then there was Juliette Greco. This perfect, petite vision of beauty, this promise of happiness, would come around to the rehearsals to listen and to focus her attention on Miles. Of course, Miles noted this and kept asking anyone around if they knew who she was. Someone said she was an existentialist, to which Miles replied, "I don't care what she is. That girl is beautiful and I want to meet her." Finally, after no one had done the proper thing and made the introductions, Miles beckoned Juliette over and she told him that while she did not like men she liked him. After that they were inseparable.

Despite her lack of English and his lack of French, they had a whirlwind affair. They communicated through ges-

Birth of the Cool sessions, but that did not lessen Miles's sarcasm or quasi-racist remarks about the success of these white musicians.

On the home front things had fallen apart as well. The more Miles got into his music, the less time he spent with Irene and the children. In truth Miles had lost interest in Irene, especially after his tryst with an artistic, independent-minded woman like Juliette Greco. Irene gave Miles a hard time about not paying attention to her and suspected he was fooling around (which he rarely did), and thinking of other women whenever he sat in their dreary Queens living room staring into space (Miles was thinking about music).

During this period, Miles spent a lot of time with a younger set of musicians—they were his age—and most of them used or dabbled in heroin. He hung out and played with Art Blakey, Sonny Rollins, Jackie McLean, Tadd Dameron, J. J. Johnson, and Dexter Gordon. Miles was particularly close to Rollins and McLean. Dexter Gordon was also a close early friend who, in Miles's words, "hipped him to the importance of looking sharp." Rollins, McLean, and sometimes Johnson and Walter Bishop, were his running buddies in the Sugarhill section of Harlem, a nice middle-class residential area where Miles passed most of his time.

At first, like most people who become junkies, Miles started off snorting, taking pinches here, inhaling longer lines there. He avoided injecting because needles scared him. Once he got over the initial effects—violently convulsive retching and the feeling of all his insides in churning, grueling turmoil—Miles savored the kick, which novelist and long-term junkie William Burroughs once compared to a bodywide orgasm.

In any case, Miles was playing in clubs all around Harlem. Afterwards, he would snort as much heroin as humanly possible, now and then mixing it with cocaine, a lethal concoction known as a "speedball." His dabbling gradually led to a higher tolerance of the drug and heavy abuse. Despite the nasty side effects of vomiting, chills, convulsions, Miles was becoming a slave to an opiate—quite a change for such a fiercely independent man.

Miles moved out on Irene Birth and the children. He had lost interest in sex in general and in her in particular. He left Irene in the care of the great jazz and blues singer Betty Carter, who pulled her through this predicament. For ever afterwards, according to Miles, Betty Carter had little, if anything, to say to him.

Heroin became for Miles, as it does for most junkies, his entire life. It became a substitute for sex. Before his addiction Miles had become something of a ladies' man. In addition to Juliette Greco, whom he adored for "her way of looking at life and her style, in and out of bed," Miles had many affairs and one-nighters with jazz groupies and even a few well-known musicians, including the singers Annie Ross and Anita O'Day. But heroin pretty much stopped all that, effectively putting a mute in his horn.

One day Miles was hanging around in his neighborhood in Queens, feeling miserable with aches, chills, a runny nose, a persistent cough. Must be a bad cold or the flu, Miles reasoned. A neighborhood hustler named Matinee happened to pass by and asked Miles what was wrong. Miles told him about how he had been going to Manhattan every day to cop coke and smack, and on this particular day he had not been able to. He also mentioned his miserable cold. Matinee looked at him as if he were a complete fool. He told Miles that what he had was not a cold but a habit. "What do you mean a habit?" Miles asked. "Your nose is running, you got chills, you weak," Matinee retorted. "You got a habit." Matinee then got Miles, free of charge, some smack, and recommended that he shoot up instead, so that the drug would last longer. Matinee showed Miles the works. Miles felt better. Thus began a four-year horror show.

A natty Miles posed for this publicity shot in the early 1950s. Despite his success, Miles was falling victim to a nasty drug habit.

On heroin Miles, like any other junkie, did anything to get his fix. If it meant hocking his horn, giving pints of blood, giving up his car, then so be it. If it meant not dressing well, indeed looking shabby in soiled, dirty clothes, then so be it. If it meant stealing or getting beat up by dealers for not paying on time, then so be it. If it meant agreeing to the harsh terms of a contract with the Prestige/Fantasy jazz label, then so be it. If it meant pimping, then so be it. If it meant getting busted in Los Angeles with buddies Dexter Gordon and Art Blakey, a jail stay, and all the subsequent bad publicity, then so be it. (Miles was acquitted in a trial in 1951, but a subsequent *Downbeat* article made it almost impossible for him to get work, hence his turning to Prestige and working for peanuts.)

If it meant stealing from one's friends, then so be it. One day Clark Terry came across Miles on the street. Miles was in a bad way. Clark decided to help his old St. Louis pal, buying him breakfast and inviting him up to his residency hotel suite. There Miles could bathe, freshen up, relax, put on some new clothes, and stay as long as he liked while Terry was away on tour. As soon as Clark left, Miles went through everything, pocketing whatever money was around and carrying whatever was not nailed down out to hock. He even stole Clark's threads.

Out of great concern for Miles, Terry called Doc Davis and told him about his son's dirty little secret. Terry offered to help in any way possible. He even forgave Miles, realizing that being in such a condition Miles was not himself. Their friendship remained firm and steadfast, although for years afterwards whenever Clark caught Miles in a bar with his money out he would help himself to it. It was their little private joke.

This stealing incident triggered Miles's first attempt at quitting junk. Out of control and looking like a bum, Miles decided something had to give. His habit was affecting his performance; his embouchure (the use of lips, tongue, and teeth in playing a wind instrument) was not what it used to be. He hit upon the solution to his drug problem: boxing. The discipline of the sport would pull him through.

A longtime boxing fan, Miles decided a little training would keep him distracted, take his mind off drugs, get his health back. He went up to Bobby McQuillen, a trainer at New York City's renowned Gleason's Gym, to see if he would take him up. McQuillen told him to beat it—he didn't train junkies. After that humiliation of having someone he respected call him a junkie to his face, Miles called his father and told him to come get him.

One night Miles and his band at the time—Jackie McLean on alto, Jimmy Heath on tenor, Percy Heath on bass, Gil Coggins on piano, and Art Blakey on drums—were playing at the Downbeat club when Doc Davis walked in and sat down in the front row. He could see how ragged his son looked. After a brief powwow with the club owner and the band, Doc took Miles down from the bandstand and spirited him back to East St. Louis. Miles later said, "I felt like a little boy again going with his daddy."

This second attempt to get the monkey off his back failed. Miles soon tired of country living and began craving heroin. It was not long before he found a few lowlifes and scored some smack, and Miles was soon sticking a needle in his arm. He began borrowing money from his father to buy drugs. He earned a little on his own, playing his horn around town, but he kept shooting up. The monkey on his back quickly ballooned into a gorilla.

Things really fell apart when his sister, Dorothy, told Doc Davis what Miles was doing with the money. Doc Davis cut him off, prompting an enormous blow-up scene in his dentistry office. In the midst of all the cursing and abuse and screaming (all on Miles's part), two men grabbed him and took him to a nearby jail in Belleville, Illinois. The "arrest" had been arranged by Doc Davis, who was also a sheriff in Belleville. The hope was that a week in a jail cell would be enough time for Miles to kick his habit, cold turkey.

Being in jail for week was an education. According to Miles he learned a lot about stealing and picking pockets from his cellmates. He also learned he did not like jail. Upon release, he believed himself cured. He had not shot up in two weeks, which he thought proof positive of having kicked the habit. In any case Miles had it under control—or so he thought. With great trepidation, Doc Davis and his second wife, Josephine, let Miles return to New York. As soon as he got back, Miles began dabbling with heroin again.

A little under the skin here, a little under there. No harm at all, Miles thought. Quickly he reassembled his band and was off and headlining again—and mainlining too. But when a junkie is high on horse, his or her behavior goes unchecked, friends and family slowly disappear, and the appetite for food, sex, and even living itself is lost. All of this happened to Miles from 1949 to 1954.

Miles sank pretty low again: borrowed clothes, borrowed horn, pimping, getting beaten up. Once again he had blown a chance to kick the habit. One day as he stood outside Birdland, the famous Broadway jazz club named after the man himself, almost nodding off, his old pal Max Roach happened by. Max was taking care of himself, had kicked his habit for good, and looked all right. He saw this pathetic carcass of a man pretending to be Miles Davis, nodding off, snot coming out of his nose, clothes dirty and soiled, and told it, "You're looking pretty good!" and slapped two crisp hundred-dollar bills in its shirt pocket. Miles was so embarrassed by this that instead of taking the money and using it to buy heroin he called his father and told him he was coming home, to really kick his habit.

Max Roach and Charlie Mingus, who were on their way to the West Coast to do some gigs in September 1953, gave Miles a lift to East St. Louis. But the stop at Doc Davis's was brief. Miles went on to California with Max and Charles. In California, Miles played a few dates at the Lighthouse, where he sat in with a number of West Coast school musicians, including Chet Baker. Miles also met his future wife, the dancer Frances Taylor, there.

Resolving again that he had to kick the habit, he returned to East St. Louis. Miles arrived a mess but with determination. After a long walk with his father through the forest, Miles holed up in a two-room guest house. There, he suffered the agonies of going cold turkey: the vomiting, the shakes, the chills, the dehumanizing feeling of being so open and vulnerable and raw, the occasional wish to die right then and there. He screamed and wailed like he was being dragged down to hell, but in truth he was being pulled out of it.

This time it worked. After a week or so in isolation, the habit was history. Miles got out of the sickroom of the guest house and into the fresh air again. He ran to his father and bear hugged him. There were tears all around and food too; Miles ate like there was no tomorrow. He made love to his girlfriend. For the first time in years, he enjoyed sex. But most important, Miles had kicked the habit the only way he knew how: his way, however arduous.

6 Golden Years

After going cold turkey, Miles went to Detroit, where he played with such local talent as Elvin Jones, Betty Carter, Yusef Lateef, Thad Jones, Tommy Flanagan, and Donald Byrd. The camaraderie was there and the heroin in Detroit was so cut and adulterated that, according to the drummer, Philly Joe Jones (who was to play in Miles's first great quintet), "You could have bought a Hershey bar and saved your money."

In time, though, Miles would have to return to his old stomping grounds, New York City. He was hesitant, naturally, because he did not want to fall into his old habits again, but he had to go back. When Miles arrived, the musical landscape in New York had changed completely. Cool jazz was all the rage. John Lewis's Modern Jazz Quartet (MJQ) was the talk of the town, as were Chet Baker (who was a white, watered-down Miles), Lennie Tristano, and George Shearing. Bird was a bloated, drugged-up mess, who, for the first time in his life, was playing ineptly if not badly.

Miles quickly re-signed with Bob Weinstock's Prestige label. Because of his prior drug bust (of which he was cleared), he was still without his cabaret card, which was necessary to play in New York City clubs. Nevertheless, on Prestige he recorded with (and often led) such musicians as Horace Silver, Art Taylor, Sonny Rollins, Thelonious Monk, and Art Blakey. He produced such masterpieces as "Walkin'," "Bemsha Swing," and "Bag's Groove." Though he and the others were working for little money, Miles learned a lot about how records are put together and how magic is created in the studio.

In addition to his work, Miles continued to follow boxing. Miles studied the then world-champion welterweight Sugar Ray Robinson, who was training at a gym on 116th Street. He and Sugar Ray knew one another from various Harlem nightspots, particularly the champ's own club. Aside from his trainer, the only other person Sugar Ray took boxing advice from was an old black fighter from an earlier era called Soldier. On those rare occasions when it looked as if Sugar Ray was losing it in the gym, was not sparring with the right intensity, or was letting it slip away in an actual title bout, he would bend his ear to Soldier's advice and then proceed to thrash his opponent.

Miles found his own Soldier in Gil Evans, who now and then offered such advice as: "Miles, you know you got a nice, open sound and tone on your trumpet. Why don't you use it more." Or Evans would call at 3 A.M. to say, "If you're ever depressed, Miles, just listen to 'Springsville'" (a wonderful tune they recorded on their *Miles Ahead* album). Or when they were recording, Evans would say, "Miles, now don't let them play that music by themselves. You play something over them, put your sound in it, too."

The struggle to free himself from his habit had even

touched Juliette Greco. In the summer of 1955 Juliette came over to act in the film version of Ernest Hemingway's *The Sun Also Rises*. Miles and Juliette had last seen one another in 1949. Their reunion did not go well. Miles showed up at her Waldorf suite and treated her in a very offhand fashion. Putting on his best pimp act, he demanded money and left to buy drugs. Miles admitted in his autobiography that all he really wanted to do was grab her and make love to her, but he was scared of his emotions, of being unable to control himself. Miles later called Juliette to explain why he had treated her so meanly. Though deeply hurt, she forgave him, and they remained very good friends and lovers for many years.

Miles later asserted that his down-and-out period had warped him to a degree. He became even more wary, suspicious, and standoffish than ever before. The Miles who turned his back on the audience, the Miles who told bores and panderers and just plain curious fans to blow was conceived and born in this period. After what he had gone through, after having been written off, exploited, and beaten up, Miles had developed an especially thick hide, metaphorically and literally speaking. Although it might have cost him potential friends and admirers, not to mention money, Miles was never going to be anyone's fool again. True, old friends—Diz, Gil, Max, Sonny Rollins, Monk, Clark Terry, and the rest—understood. They knew the real Miles Davis.

Miles's ideas on music began to change again about this time. Although he did not want to repeat what he had done in his bebop phase, neither did he want to go much farther with his own contribution to the music—cool jazz—which for him was now too sanitized and too associated with white musicians. Miles wanted something fast, hard, and funky, like the stuff he had heard in Detroit. Ideally he wanted a combination of the best of bebop and cool. Miles even had in mind certain musicians, notably Percy Heath on bass, Kenny Clarke on drums (for his brush work), and Sonny Rollins on tenor. He couldn't get Rollins because he was going through an ugly dope period and was in and out of jail and rehab constantly.

Miles's first choice for a pianist had always been Bud Powell, but in the mid-1950s Powell was broken man, living and working fitfully in Paris. Miles's sister, Dorothy, put him on to the music of pianist Ahmad Jamal, whose keynotes were (and still are) understatement, lyricism, and an effortless, elegantly imaginative use of space. Jamal quietly influenced a whole school of pianists. He had an enormous impact on Miles in the 1950s, and therefore on such pianists as Red Garland and Bill Evans, both of whom played in Miles's 1950s groups.

On March 12, 1955, Charlie Parker collapsed and died in the Fifth Avenue apartment of the jazz-loving aristocrat Baroness Pannonica de Koenigswarter. The coroner who examined Bird at first guessed his age to be between 65 and 70—he was 35. Bird's death left a void in jazz that was not easily filled. Everyone knew Bird was in bad shape, drunk all the time, constantly strung out on heroin, and not even playing all that well. His death nonetheless came as a shock. About the only good to result from Bird's demise was a climatic change among a great many of his followers and admirers—they realized that they had to stop shooting up or suffer the same fate as Bird.

Miles was as stunned as everybody else, and although he had not been particularly close to Bird for years, he was still angry and hurt by the waste. As he put it, "It just made me sad that Bird had died like he did, because, man he was a genius and he had so much he could have given. But that's the way life is. Bird was a greedy motherfucker and never did know when to stop, and that's what killed him—his greed."

Ahmad Jamal practices his art in 1952.
Jamal's lyrical and understated style greatly
influenced Miles.

In the summer of 1955, Miles's career took a turn for the better when he played as a last-minute substitute at the very first Newport Jazz Festival. That first festival, which featured such greats as Louis Armstrong, Count Basie, Woody Herman, and Dave Brubeck, was an unqualified success. But it was Miles who stole the show with his stellar lead in an all-star pickup band on "Now's the Time" (played in tribute to Bird) and, above all, using his mute on "'Round Midnight," the Monk signature tune that only a few years back had given him so much trouble. After the number ended he received a long standing ovation. Even his fellow musicians Gerry Mulligan, Connie Kay, Monk, Percy Heath, and Zoot Sims knew that Miles had done something special. Miles was back, and everyone knew it.

Everybody wanted Miles too. Amidst all the flashes from cameras and the roars of approval from the audience, Miles was besieged by record executives and hustlers wanting his name on a contract. At the party given afterward by the wealthy Lorillard family at their splendid mansion, Miles was approached by the hostess, Elaine Lorillard, who had cofounded the festival with her husband, Louis. She brought over a group of revelers to meet Miles. "Oh, this is the boy who played so beautifully. What's your name?" Lorillard asked. Miles shot back, "Fuck you, and I ain't no fucking boy! My name is Miles Davis, and you'd better remember that if you ever want to talk to me." With that he stormed out. Miles never again played Newport.

Miles was still with Prestige and getting paid very little. He felt some gratitude to owner Bob Weinstock, the only man in the business who gave him work when he was down and out. But after he finished his contractual obligations to Prestige, Miles signed with Columbia for big bucks. Now all he needed was a band. Miles found his

Ahmad Jamal–style pianist in the formidable Texan Red Garland. His drummer was Philly Joe Jones, one of the great innovators of the jazz drums in the bebop age. Philly's great contribution to jazz was his patented Philly lick, a kind of rim shot that comes a bit after the end of a solo; very soon every bandleader wanted his drummer to do the Philly lick. The bassist was Paul Chambers, a 20-year-old from Detroit. Miles discovered Chambers in the Motor City and knew right away he was witnessing genius.

The problem was finding a saxophonist. Miles wanted Sonny Rollins, but just at the point when he was going to hire Rollins, Sonny left New York to kick his habit for good. Miles then heard Julian "Cannonball" Adderly, a high school music teacher from Florida, play at Café Bohemia and was bedazzled. When Miles heard the alto's ripping runs and his down-and-dirty blues, his jaw dropped all the way to floor. Miles introduced himself after the set was done, and they became very fast friends. On top of being an outstanding musician, Cannonball was a great guy. Unfortunately, he wasn't too interested in Miles's band; he had to return to Florida to the security of his teaching job.

Philly Joe came to the rescue, talking up his fellow Philadelphian John Coltrane. Miles wasn't excited at first. He had played with Coltrane before and thought that he was a good musician but nothing extraordinary. More than anything else, however, Miles had been annoyed by Trane's demeanor, which was very serious, soft -spoken, only interested in music, and always inquisitive. "Why did we play it like this? Why did the piano come in just then? What am I supposed to be feeling?" Trane needed to know everything about the music, whereas Miles preferred to go on feeling and intellect, with few rehearsals and the barest of musical sketches as signposts. He didn't want to lose the freshness of the first take or first few takes.

But this time around, when Trane sat in with the band,

Miles was astounded by what he heard. Trane had become a monster. He was exactly the right hornman for the band. All that awaited them was greatness.

The new quintet was an instant success. Their records, all superb, sold like hotcakes, and lines formed around the block at the clubs they played. And at some of these clubs, such as Birdland or the Café Bohemia, the quintet drew a very fashionable crowd indeed: Richard Burton and Claire Bloom, Elizabeth Taylor and Mike Todd, Eddie Fisher and Debbie Reynolds, Frank Sinatra, Ava Gardner, Tony Bennett, Lena Horne, Dorothy Dandridge, Marlon Brando, James Dean, and Sugar Ray Robinson. Miles was also meeting and associating with a heady literary crowd, writers and poets such as William Burroughs, Allen Ginsberg, Leroi Jones (later Amira Baraka), and Jack Kerouac.

Unfortunately, heroin was eating up the band from within. Ironically, Miles was the only one who was clean. Trane, Red, Paul, and Philly were all junkies and heavy drinkers. Miles drank with them and occasionally snorted coke if he was working long hours. The quintet could really cook, but too many times someone on the bandstand, maybe Red or Trane, would nod off when sitting out. Not only was this damaging to the music and to discipline, and not the least to themselves, but Miles looked bad by association. People began to wonder whether he was still on his high horse.

Heroin wasn't a big problem for Philly Joe. He was funny, hip, slick, and his street smarts and survival skills helped him get through despite his stupid habit. With Red Garland, addiction was not a pretty sight. He might show up at a gig in a dirty suit or look like he had slept in his clothes for a week. Paul Chambers would run up enormous bar tabs, on top of shooting up. But it was Trane who was, for Miles, truly a figure of pathos. Serious, gentle, rather sweet in a way, and devoted to his girlfriend, Naima

The Miles Davis quintet plays at the 1958 Newport Jazz
Festival. From left to right are: Bill Evans, Jimmy Cobb,
Paul Chambers, Miles, and John Coltrane.

(whom he married and wrote a famous hymn to), Trane's self-destruction was a sad sight.

Miles found himself shelling out more and more money to keep the band relatively straight. He paid their tabs, occasionally gave advances so the guys could buy drugs, and saw to it that there was no trouble. It was a tall order, being bandleader, mother hen, good cop/bad cop, and pay-master. Miles was actually losing money, and he finally blew his top. One night, after a gig at Café Bohemia, he slapped Trane. Thelonious Monk interceded, saying, "Man, as much as you play on saxophone, you don't have to take nothing like that; you can come and play with me anytime. And you, Miles, you shouldn't be hitting on him like that." Miles told Monk to mind his own business and fired Trane right then and there. After the Bohemia gig ended, Miles broke up the band and went to Paris to play at a jazz festi-val. Trane joined Monk's band.

In Paris, Miles renewed his affair with Juliette Greco, hung out with Sartre again, and generally lived the good life as it can only be lived there. Miles and Juliette, with members of the Modern Jazz Quartet tagging along, were out one night and bumped into Bud Powell and his wife, Buttercup, at a jazz club. Miles and Bud carried on like long lost brothers, and after a time Bud announced to the party that he was going to play. After a wonderful, rippling start, his playing suddenly veered off course and became badly disjointed. There was silence and shock all around. Bud knew it, and trying to put on his best face, he stumbled through an impromptu ending (he had been playing "Nice Work If You Can Get It"). After what seemed a moment of eternal silence, there was stunned applause (no one knew how to respond), and then Miles saved the evening by get-ting up and putting his arm around Bud and saying in a low voice loud enough so everyone could hear, "Bud, now you know you shouldn't be playing when you've been drinking like you have; now you know that, don't you?" Everything returned to normal, Bud's feelings were spared, his wife's tears stifled. Miles was deeply affected by this episode and never forgot it.

After returning from Paris, Miles reassembled the band, Trane included, but, the junk problems continued. It turned out that Philly was the evil influence in the band, especially on Trane. Fed-up, Miles fired and rehired Philly and Trane and Red; Paul Chambers was the only one who remained anchored in the quintet, even though he, too, was a junkie and near alcoholic.

Miles often lost his temper in this period, and it's easy to see why. His short fuse, however, cost him his voice. Just after the quintet had first been formed, Miles had had an operation to remove a noncancerous growth on his larynx. Not too long after he left the hospital he bumped into a record producer who was trying to sign him to a ridiculous contract. Miles, who was not supposed to talk for at least ten days, got angry, shouted at his persistent suitor and permanently damaged his voice box. At first Miles was very self-conscious about his new voice, a low, raspy whisper, but he soon grew accustomed to it; in time it only added to his mystique.

In May 1957, Miles exchanged his trumpet for the flügelhorn and went into the studio with Gil Evans to record *Miles Ahead*, one of the greatest large-ensemble jazz albums ever. Gil and Miles had been close ever since *Birth of the Cool*, but this was only their second collaboration. *Miles Ahead* changed the sound of the big band, making it new. Three weeks after he had bought the recording, Dizzy Gillespie asked Miles for another copy because he had worn his out after playing it so often—perhaps the highest compliment of all.

Later in 1957, one of Miles's long-standing wishes came true: Cannonball Adderley agreed to be in the quin-

Miles practices with a muted horn in 1958.

tet, making it a sextet. So Miles, Trane, Cannonball, Paul Chambers, Red Garland, and Philly went on a tour called Jazz for Moderns, which closed at New York City's prestigious Carnegie Hall. They also went into the studio and recorded one of the masterpieces of jazz, *Milestones* (1958), covering such gems as "Miles," Sid's Ahead," and Monk's "Straight, No Chaser."

After the powerful debut of his new group, Miles rushed off to Paris again to play some dates. He hooked up again with Juliette Greco, who introduced him to the brilliant French New Wave film director Louis Malle. An admirer of Miles and his music, Malle commissioned him to write the score for his latest picture, *L'Ascenseur pour l'Echafaud* (*Elevator to the Gallows*), starring Jeanne Moreau. The film, a murder mystery, was a big success, as was Miles's music, especially a tune entitled "Green Dolphin Street."

When Miles got back to New York, the sextet took off again, like a jet plane. With Cannonball's blues-rooted alto and Trane's harmonic, chordal way of constructing and deconstructing solos, which was cut into and topped by Miles's straightforward, less-is-more style, the sextet ripped up everything in sight. The dimensions of the band had changed, however. Everyone in it was now a "star," and Trane, off drugs, was clearly developing his own following, much as Miles had when he played with Bird. In fact, Trane and Cannonball were recording albums on their own. Trane eventually became one of the most important figures in the history of jazz and American popular music, a true innovator and explorer of the limits of the form.

Although not nearly as innovative or revolutionary as Trane, Cannonball nonetheless made many wonderful recordings, among the best jazz/blues albums of the 1960s and 1970s. For some reason, he has remained a marginal figure in the history of the music. Despite introducing such musicians as his brother, the cornetist Nat Adderly, and the pianist and composer Joe Zawinul to listeners, Cannonball Adderly has yet to receive his proper due.

Now that he was off junk, Trane spent all his spare time with his wife or practicing his music. His playing, within and outside the context of the band, became wilder, more stretched out, and at times almost cacophonous. He played longer and longer solos, never repeating his solos from nights previous. Every gig became an essay in redefining himself and refining his art. One time after a nearly 15-minute solo, Trane joked to Miles that once he got started improvising his solo he did not know how to stop. "Why don't you take the horn out your mouth?" was Miles's curt suggestion.

Not too long later, in 1958, Red Garland walked out on the band. Miles hired a white pianist named Bill Evans. His classical training and semi–Ahmad Jamal touch were just what the doctor ordered, because Miles was going in a different direction in his music. Evans, like Trane, was a quiet, fundamentally serious character.

During this period, Miles began living with Frances Taylor. Like Juliette Greco, Frances had a definite influence on Miles's art and life. A rising star in the dance world, Frances introduced Miles to African music. Like Juliette, she also was an artist with an independent mind, intelligent, and self-confident. Miles eventually married her (his first legal marriage), but like a great many men of that generation, he could not handle his wife having a career, so he did what he could to stifle it. He also could not stop chasing skirts, especially when he was on the road, and when he got mad he would hit her. Nonetheless, as he said in his autobiography, Miles regarded Frances as the best woman he ever loved and regretted how he had treated her. (Tiring of Miles's willful self-destruction and numerous infidelities, she would walk out on him in 1965 and divorce him in 1968.)

In 1958 Miles hooked up again with Gil Evans. This time they undertook the recording of George Gershwin's masterpiece *Porgy and Bess*. As with *Miles Ahead* and *Birth of the Cool*, their collaboration was brilliant. *Porgy and Bess* belongs alongside such past triumphs as *Miles Ahead*, *Birth of the Cool*, *Milestones*, *'Round About Midnight*, and "Green Dolphin Street."

But things were changing with the band. Trane was itching to do his own music. Bill Evans wanted to move on and, after only nine months, did so, forming his own very influential trio. Philly Joe's opiate antics finally drove Miles to fire him for good. He was replaced with the excellent Jimmy Cobb. Finally, Cannonball wanted to leave to form a group with his brother.

Despite the tension in the band, Miles got them all together in early 1959 to record *Kind of Blue*. With such classics as "All Blues," "Flamenco Sketches" "Freddie Freeloader," and the rest, the album was a masterpiece, an instant classic, a seminal recording in the history of the music, the highest development of the modal, progressive tradition of jazz. *Kind of Blue*, like *Birth of the Cool* nine years earlier, changed the landscape of jazz. Every musician was touched by it, took from it, or reacted to it. For Miles, Trane, and Cannonball, *Kind of Blue* was the end of the line. All that remained were dates and other contractual obligations that had to be met.

Then in the summer of 1959 something happened to Miles that embittered him for good: he was beaten up by the police. One evening at Birdland, where Miles and his band were playing for the Voice of America and the Armed Forces Day broadcast, Miles went out to walk a pretty young woman to a cab, a chivalrous act that did not go unnoticed by a cop on the beat. The reason he noticed was because the woman was white. After she left the cop came by and asked Miles to move along. Miles, irritated by the

The marquee of the Black Hawk announces Miles's appearance at the club.

cop's nasty tone, replied, "Move on, for what? I'm working downstairs. That's my name up there, Miles Davis." The cop repeated his demand and threatened to run Miles in. Miles would not give ground, so the cop told him he was going to arrest him. By this time a crowd had gathered. The cop stumbled as he was reaching for his handcuffs, and an undercover cop emerged from the crowd and blindsided Miles with a club. There was blood everywhere. To prevent a riot, the cops hustled Miles off to the nearest precinct.

The next day, Miles found he had a lot of friends and supporters, black and white. His beating and arrest became national news. Dorothy Kilgallen, the newspaper columnist and Miles's friend, had been inside the club. She caught the tail end of the disturbance and, like everyone else on the scene, was horrified and angry. She wrote a column condemning the police for wrongful arrest and brutality. His beating and arrest became national news. The charges against Miles for loitering and resisting arrest were dropped.

Shortly after this incident, the band finally broke up when Cannonball left. Something was lost, a vital ingredient, and Miles was, in truth, running out of ideas. He needed a rest, so late in 1959, he visited a friend in Los Angeles, the studio bass player Joe Montdragon. Joe introduced Miles to the music of Spanish composer Joaquin Rodrigo and in particular to his famous *Concierto de Aranjuez*. Miles was inspired by the music's deep feeling, its strong melody, its strange melancholic strain. Upon returning to New York, he got Gil Evans to listen to a recording of it, which led to their most complex and involved project yet, *Sketches of Spain*.

Sketches of Spain contained some of the most beautiful and evocative music Miles ever recorded. Although the core of the album is the *Concierto*, Gil and Miles added a number of folk tunes, transcribed and arranged by Gil and performed with just the right intuition and feeling by Miles. *Sketches of Spain* turned out to be Miles's most popular recording to date, a critical and financial success. But Miles was so burnt out that he claims never to have listened to *Sketches* after it was finished. His monster sextet was history. The band was a barely a quintet now and they were starting to repeat themselves. And the 1960s stared Miles in the face. What was ahead? What was there left to say or play? Miles did not know nor did he seem to care.

Seven

What Is This Thing Called Free Jazz?

The 1960s started badly for Miles. The decade began with the band touring Europe. Although the band slayed them in France, Germany, and England, there was much dissension within. Trane had inadvertently told a reporter that he was leaving the band because he wanted to do his own music, and that Wayne Shorter, a tenor in Art Blakey's Jazz Messengers, was to be his replacement. Miles, angered by Trane's hanging dirty linen in public, ripped into him.

A day or two before the tour ended, Miles and Trane made up, and there was peace once again in the family. Miles went out and bought Trane a soprano saxophone in a Paris music shop. Trane was enthralled with his new toy, fell in love with it immediately, and set out to master it. He would become as famous for his soprano playing as his tenor, indeed becoming the second great exponent of the instrument after Sidney Bechet, who played it more like a clarinet.

After Trane left the band in May 1960, Miles tried to get

Wayne Shorter to join, but he had been made musical director of the Jazz Messengers. So Miles brought in his good friend Jimmy Heath, a fine tenor from Philadelphia. But because of the conditions of his parole—Heath had done time for drugs—he couldn't venture beyond a 60-mile radius of Philadelphia. It was a shame because Heath knew Miles's book and was an excellent player.

After that Miles had a succession of tenors. The first was his friend Sonny Stitt, who unfortunately couldn't play in the style Miles wanted. Then there was Hank Mobley, another fine if unspectacular musician whom Miles treated with great contempt on and off the bandstand. When Hank was playing, Miles's solos became noticeably shorter and shriller and were punctuated by his hasty departure from the bandstand. He apparently didn't want to be anywhere near Mobley. Sonny Rollins also sat in for a while, but he left to do his own music. Legend has it that he would hang around high up in the girders of the Brooklyn Bridge, practicing incessantly.

In addition to the constant turnover at saxophone, Miles had to deal with the rhythm section: Wynton Kelly, Paul Chambers, and Jimmy Cobb wanted out. They were bored with the music and, like a great many other musicians and listeners around that time, were anxious to experiment with the new wave in jazz—free jazz.

In 1960, a young alto from Texas, Ornette Coleman, and his sidekick, the trumpeter Don Cherry, hit the New York music scene like a hurricane. Their music, which was often atonal (a nice way of saying unstructured, chordless, or just plain noisy), was an attempt to redefine jazz, going purely with the emotion or spirit of the moment, never mind how it comes out or how it sounds. What the music may have lacked in niceties of structure, melody, or harmony, it more than made up for in sheer visceral and auditory energy. No one could remain indifferent to it. Free jazz excited—or

During a 1959 gig at the Music Inn, Ornette Coleman blasts away on his plastic saxophone. The key figure in the genesis of free jazz, Coleman turned the music world upside down.

infuriated—listeners, critics, and musicians alike. It resembled nothing that had come before it, or so it seemed. Miles asserted that there was nothing original in free jazz, that playing free form, bouncing ideas off one another, had been done before and had been done better. True enough, but audiences have short memories.

But what really made Miles mad was the praise—a lot of it stupid, misinformed, and ahistorical—lavished on what he felt was mere novelty. He was miffed the chic crowd that had sat in studied reverence of his group at the Café Bohemia and the Vanguard were now showing up to see Ornette and his band blow. Classical composer and conductor Leonard Bernstein, who should have known better, was in such a lather over Ornette and Don that one hot night he jumped up and solemnly declared, "This is the greatest thing that has ever happened to jazz!" Miles also didn't care for what he regarded as Coleman's arrogance in randomly picking up instruments, the trumpet and violin specifically, and playing them in public. Because Ornette had never studied trumpet or violin, it showed a contempt for musical discipline and learning and for musicians who have spent years mastering these particular instruments.

On a personal level, Miles got along with Coleman and actually liked Don Cherry, who was cheerful and easygoing. Miles even went so far as to play with them in their style, but he got nothing out of it. He did come to like Ornette's later music, which developed structurally, harmonically, and melodically.

The one musician of the free jazz movement who really got under Miles's skin was the classically trained pianist Cecil Taylor, who was doing on piano, usually solo, what Ornette and Don were doing in small group settings. Miles thought Cecil Taylor showy and pretentious, and he never tried to mask his disdain. In one famous incident, Miles, Sarah Vaughan, and Dizzy Gillespie got dragged into a club to hear Taylor play. Upon hearing Cecil's customary banshee wailing and moaning on the keys, Miles laughed so hard and so much that he got up and left. Everyone noticed, especially Cecil Taylor. Years later, when asked what he thought of Miles as a trumpet player, Taylor icily replied, "He plays all right for a millionaire."

Miles's attitude towards free jazz was not all that off base; it really only appealed to a small coterie within the larger jazz audience, which was not that large to begin with. Free jazz drove off many listeners who might have turned to jazz as an alternative to the really popular mainstream music of the day, rock 'n' roll and pop.

Not all of Miles's problems during this period concerned music. In the early 1960s, he was diagnosed as having sickle-cell anemia, a genetic disorder that distorts the shape of red blood cells. Miles developed such severe arthritis—brought on by sickle-cell anemia—that he often had to be put in hospital. He began combining his medication with huge quantities of alcohol and cocaine, which led to troubles with his wife, Frances. Though seemingly on top of the world—he was the first person ever interviewed by *Playboy* magazine, he had spreads in *Life* and *Ebony*, he was making at least $200,000 a year, he had a great pad on West 77th Street, and he drove a slick Ferrari—Miles was depressed with his music. Amid the disorienting swirl of drugs and the pain caused by sickle-cell anemia, he lashed out at Frances for trivial things. And, of course, Miles made matters worse with his constant skirt chasing.

At one point Max Roach got it into his head that Miles was messing around with his wife, the singer Abbey Lincoln. It was totally untrue, but Max went out in search of Miles and found him at Sugar Ray's in Harlem. There he confronted Miles, accused him of sleeping with his wife, and tried to pick a fight. Miles tried to explain the truth to Max, but he kept coming and Miles knocked him down.

Sporting his hippest Sixties threads,
Miles hangs out in his New York City apartment.

The two old friends had to be separated. It was an emotionally wrenching experience for Miles, and in his autobiography he admitted to returning home to Frances and crying "like a baby in her arms that night, all night." Alcohol had done to Max what heroin had done to Miles. Miles understood this and let bygones be bygones, and eventually the two men made up.

Miles also faced family problems. His mother, Cleota Henry Davis, had been diagnosed with cancer. Her illness brought mother and son closer together before she died quietly in 1964. Far more upsetting to Miles was the decline and death of his father, Doc Davis. In 1960, Doc Davis got hit by a train and was never quite the same. He developed palsy, had trouble concentrating, and at times slurred his speech. But being a proud, obstinate man, Doc Davis refused help of any kind. He insisted he was going to come back good as new and would start working again in no time. It was never to be. One evening, during a gig in Kansas City, J. J. Johnson, who was playing with Miles at the time, broke the news to Miles: his father had died suddenly back in East St. Louis. Three days earlier Doc Davis had given Miles a letter, but Miles, in a hurry to get to the airport, had handed it to Frances without reading it. Now Miles asked to see the letter. In it his father had written, "A few days after you read this I'll be dead, so take care of yourself, Miles. I truly loved you, and you made me proud." For a while Miles was eaten up with guilt for not having read the letter when he should have, for not having been by his father's side. Doc Davis's funeral was an enormous affair. Dignitaries of all kinds—black, white, doctors, lawyers, rich, poor—came to pay their respects.

During all these personal crises, the music was not happening for Miles. He had become quite passé in the phony age of free jazz. He and Gil Evans collaborated on yet another album, *Quiet Nights* (1962), an attempt by their record company, Columbia, to cash in on the bossa nova craze. *Quiet Nights* was a commercial and critical failure, but it was more Columbia's fault than Miles's or Gil's. After this debacle they decided to take a break. The two men were going in different directions anyway: Gil was further developing modal and progressive jazz forms with a big ensemble; Miles was going around in circles. Things finally fell apart for Miles musically when Wynton Kelly and Paul Chambers left to form their own group. Jimmy Cobb soon followed. Miles was now entirely without a band.

Miles began putting together a new band. The first person he hired was the tenor George Coleman, a cool, elegant stylist. Next came the bassist, Ron Carter, who came recommended by Paul Chambers. Carter was alternating between his studies at the prestigious Eastman School of Music and playing in Art Farmer's group. With Farmer's blessing and armed with his degree from Eastman, Carter joined Davis.

The next discovery is arguably Miles's greatest, 17-year-old drummer Tony Williams, who was playing in Jackie McLean's band. Tony Williams, as Miles put it, was the fire, the creative spark. Everything, the band's direction and sound, revolved around his endless waves of sound. There wasn't anything Tony Williams couldn't do: he had Klook's brushwork, Elvin Jones's harmonic imagination, Art Blakey's polyrhythms, Max Roach's endurance and timing, and Philly Joe Jones's inimitable swing. Indeed, if a perfect drummer could be assembled, he would bear a striking resemblance to Tony Williams, a true titan and innovator.

Finding a pianist was the next task. At first Miles wanted Victor Feldman, a slick, swinging English musician, but Feldman was making more money doing film and television work, so he declined Miles's offer. Two of his tunes, however, "Seven Steps to Heaven" and "Joshua," jazz standards now, were recorded by the band on its debut album,

Seven Steps to Heaven (1963). Miles eventually settled on Herbie Hancock. Interestingly enough, when this second great quintet is discussed Herbie Hancock (as well as George Coleman) is usually not mentioned in the same breath as Ron Carter, Tony Williams, or Wayne Shorter (who was to replace Coleman). That's unfair because Hancock is a multifaceted, innovative musician. Hancock's understated, at times percussive, punctuating approach to the piano quickly became something akin to musical shorthand for a great many other pianists, then and now.

Finally, Miles's band was ready, and they sounded great together. And for once Miles did not have to set the tone; his sidemen were almost all younger than him, and they rejuvenated and pushed him, especially Tony Williams. It was through the influence of Tony Williams, Ron Carter, and Herbie Hancock that Miles allowed the structures of free jazz to seep into his style and approach. They all loved Ornette Coleman and John Coltrane, and even saxophonist Archie Shepp.

But because of these differences, which were essential George Coleman, however, was resistant to free-form playing, a stance that annoyed his bandmates, Williams in particular. Because of his arthritis, there were times when Miles could not make it, and George was the only horn. On those occasions, the band played far-out and all-over-the-place free jazz, a practice that George complained about to Miles. Tony Williams came to dislike Coleman's playing, which he regarded as too slick, too polished. One evening, just to show them he could do it too, Coleman played really free, producing a Trane and Ornette jag that stunned the others.

ly philosophical, the quintet could not last in its present form. Something had to give, and after a concert at Philharmonic Hall to benefit various civil rights groups, George Coleman quit. The tenor chair was empty again. That final concert turned out to be one of the best live recordings Miles ever made, and the music that night was released on two albums: *My Funny Valentine* (1964) and *Four & More* (1964).

Tony and the others urged Miles to hire Eric Dolphy, another standard-bearer of free jazz, but he was never seriously considered. Miles couldn't stand the way he played. He also rejected Archie Shepp, of whom Miles said, "He couldn't play, and I wasn't going to stand up there with this no-playing motherfucker." Tony pushed for the talented fellow Bostonian Sam Rivers. Rivers came in briefly and accompanied the group to Japan. But, as with Cannonball Adderly, Miles finally got his wish: Wayne Shorter, who had first been recommended by Coltrane, left the Jazz Messengers and was quickly hired by Miles. So desirous was Miles to have him in the band that he sent Shorter a first-class ticket to get him to the reconstituted quintet's first gig, the Hollywood Bowl, on time and in style.

8 Old Dog, New Tricks

Miles's new quintet hit the ground running. And just like his monster group in the 1950s, this quintet was an instant success. Now that may not seem odd, but in 1964 the latest rages—rock, pop, and rhythm and blues—were shoving jazz out of clubs and off records. Once it had been Elvis, Chuck Berry, Little Richard, Jerry Lee Lewis, and Pat Boone doing the shoving; now it was the Beatles, the Beach Boys, Jan and Dean, the Rolling Stones, and the Supremes. But Miles and a few other jazz performers, Trane and singers like Ella Fitzgerald, were able to survive.

The new quintet prospered because it worked as a unit, even after they had all become stars. Miles was the elder statesman, the leader, the inspiration of the quintet. His sidemen even called him Mr. Davis, a deferential habit that never failed to amuse him. It amused him because Miles had nothing but the highest regard and confidence in this quintet, even more so than in his 1950s group. Wayne, Ron, Herbie, and Tony were so professional, creative, and in synch that

Miles really had little to do. If anything, they lit a fire under him. He could not sit back and relax with this bunch. Every night they reinvented his book, were constantly stretching, bringing in the concepts of free jazz in a way that actually had structure and discipline. They could break or bend the rules because they knew the rules. Because of this, the quintet played with a high degree of intuition tinged with an element of creative tension and restlessness.

Wayne Shorter, a free player who knew how far to go without sounding ridiculous, was the ideas man in the quintet. He was the composer and conceptualizer of most of its tunes. According to Miles, Shorter was the only person he knew who could write like Bird—apparently it was the way he notated the beat. Under Miles, Shorter blossomed as a composer in a way that he never had under Art Blakey. What he did in the quintet came to full fruition later in the group he founded with Joe Zawinul—the immensely influential and popular Weather Report. Shorter is one of the most significant figures in jazz to emerge in the 1960s and arguably one of its two or three best composers.

The virtues of Herbie Hancock and Ron Carter need little reemphasis. They were the anchors, never dropping the beat. Carter, unfortunately, has not received as much attention or press as his colleagues, an unjust oversight. Real jazz connoisseurs know his true value as the quintessential musician's musician and consummate pro. Hancock was never at a loss for chords or notes. He absorbed everything and never lacked ideas or improvisations. Sometimes, according to Miles, he didn't always know how to lay out, "like someone who will drink and drink until the whole bottle is gone just because it's there." Miles kidded that sometimes when he left the bandstand he would fake chopping off Herbie's hands.

The prime mover in the band was undoubtedly Tony Williams. He was simply phenomenal. Not only was his

The Miles Davis Quintet performs at Shelley's, a Los Angeles club, in 1968.

timing impeccable, but his uncanny ability to come up with new rhythm schemes every night pushed the band to new heights and directions. Miles and Wayne, the two horns, had to react to everything he did, and Miles in particular had to start practicing again, a habit that he had dropped many years earlier.

So adept was this quintet that on those nights when Miles could not make it, they easily carried on without him. They were so good that fans still paid top dollar to see them without Miles. And there were an increasing number of evenings when Miles could not play, so painful was arthritis and bursitis at times. Miles didn't help matters any; he constantly drank alcohol and used cocaine, which caused him frightening hallucinations and heart palpitations.

Miles also had a hip ailment. Twice it had to be operated on, and it was eventually replaced. He spent August 1965 in bed recuperating. He was also stricken with a liver infection, perhaps caused by all the drinking and other extracurricular activities he indulged in over the years. Those extracurricular activities contributed to the break up of Miles's marriage to Frances Taylor. Their marriage had also suffered because he refused to have children with her; he already had three kids (Cheryl, Gregory, and Miles Dewey Davis IV) and Frances had one by a previous marriage.

Around this time, Miles met the actress Cicely Tyson. Cicely had heard through the grapevine of Miles's marital troubles and thought she might be able to help him forget Frances. She found out that Miles liked taking afternoon walks in Riverside park near his West 77th Street apartment. One day when Miles went to the park, Cicely was there, making the meeting appear accidental. Miles allowed her into his life, and she began slowly nursing him back into the land of the living, getting him off hard booze and cocaine.

In July 1967, music changed once again. John Coltrane

died of liver cancer. Like the death of Bird 12 years earlier, which had devastated bebop, Trane's death left an enormous vacuum in the free jazz movement, which he, more than anyone else, had inspired. In the last year or so of his life, Trane had taken a different course with his music that was more spiritual and transcendent. His album *A Love Supreme* (1964) represents the pinnacle of his quest.

Miles, like everyone else, was shocked and depressed by Trane's death. Although he was not wild about Trane's music (especially the more far-out, free music found on *Ascension*), he loved and respected the man "because not only was he a great and beautiful musician, he was a kind and spiritual person." But, as with Bird, "he was greedy about living and his art—especially about drugs and alcohol—and it killed him in the end."

Changing, progressing, not standing still—those were the things always on Miles's mind. He hated repeating himself, and now after four brilliant years with his quintet, a period that rivals the glory years of 1955–59, he was doing just that. Never mind the sell-out concerts worldwide and such masterpieces as *ESP* (1965), *Sorcerer* (1965), *Miles Smiles* (1966), *Nefertiti* (1967), *Miles in the Sky* (1968), and *Filles de Kilimanjaro* (1968), all of which are classics. Even perfection can get dull, and, if not perfect, the current quintet was close to it. What Miles now wanted was a guitar sound and a stronger, more distinct bass line, a bit funkier perhaps. Miles was listening to a lot of South Side blues in Chicago, greats like Muddy Waters and B. B. King, and he felt that it was it time to return to the beginning. Back to basics. Back to the blues. Back to grit, to feeling, to blood, sweat, soil, and tears.

Nine
Miles Runs the Voodoo Down

Change was in the air in 1968. The Vietnam War was at its height, peaking with the Tet Offensive in the spring. Czechoslovakia attempted a quiet transformation from being a hard-line communist state to becoming a fairly open one; it was crushed by Soviet tanks. In Paris, New York, Boston, and points elsewhere, middle-class students played at revolution. They took drugs, listened to loud music, had sex with whomever they wanted, and dropped out of school. Civil rights leader Martin Luther King Jr. was assassinated in Memphis, sparking race riots nationwide. Senator Robert F. Kennedy, seeking to become the Democratic Party's presidential nominee, was gunned down in Los Angeles after winning the California primary. Republican Richard M. Nixon was elected president.

Amid this social upheaval, music changed. It had been changing all decade long, with the growth of rhythm and blues and rock and roll, but in 1968 the sounds of these popular musical forms had a grittier edge to them. The Beatles became psychedelic, the Rolling Stones took on a satanic edge, and black power was reflected in the songs of James Brown and Sly and the Family Stone. Jimi Hendrix emerged as the guitar hero of the day, changing forever the sound and role of the electric guitar in popular music.

Although content with the way his brilliant quintet had shaped up, Miles Davis was again restless. He began looking for the next big thing. Commercial considerations, naturally, played some part in his soul searching. Jazz in the 1960s had fallen on hard times because young listeners, and seemingly everyone else, had turned to rhythm and blues and rock music. Even though Columbia had always made money off Miles's albums, the label raked in considerably more with its rock, pop, and rhythm-and-blues records.

Because of this dramatic change in the recording industry, Columbia began to reconsider the manner in which they treated Miles. He had sold between 60,000 and 100,000 records a release, excellent for a jazz artist, but when such one-hit wonders as the Strawberry Alarm Clock could sell as many as 250,000, Columbia began to wonder why they should be so deferential to Miles. Why should they shell out a guaranteed $200,000 a year whether he earns it or not? And other little checks here and there when he demands it? So went the bottom-line reasoning. Columbia suggested to Miles that he needed to get in the swim, to become a little more of a showman, to lighten up. Miles had a fit when they asked him to sell out and nearly sued Columbia. But, fortunately for everyone concerned, not the least Miles, nothing legal transpired. Miles was, as usual, one step ahead of the boss man.

In 1968 Miles was listening to the music young people were listening to and digging it. And he was seeing a lot of an attractive young rhythm-and-blues singer named Betty

Davis (who was also known as Betty Mabry). Miles's marriage to Frances Taylor had officially ended. Although he was somewhat involved with actress Cicely Tyson, he was not serious about it. He admitted in his autobiography that Cicely never attracted him the way Frances Taylor or Juliette Greco had.

Betty Mabry got Miles listening to the new sounds. She also began to change the way he dressed, making him throw out his Italian-cut suits and sharp Brooks Brothers and Paul Stuart threads and replacing them with a younger, quasi-African look—dashikis, bell bottoms, studded belts, and such. Miles looked ridiculous, considering how old he was. The 42-year-old grandfather was no longer leading a charge but merely following the herd.

But before all that happened Miles had noted, with undisguised pleasure, the piano work and compositions of Joe Zawinul in Cannonball and Nat Adderly's band. Zawinul was playing a Fender Rhodes, the first electric piano, the sound of which was pure and clean and appealed to Miles immeasurably. He had to have one in his band, and maybe Joe Zawinul, too.

Miles had also noted, like most everyone else in jazz, the enormous popularity of the tenor saxophonist Charles Lloyd. Although not a particularly gifted instrumentalist, Lloyd was an innovator who brought a softer, more laid-back sound to jazz, combining Coltrane's message of universal love and sympathy with the carefree attitudes of pop and folk music and hippies. Charles Lloyd also introduced two musicians who were to have a big impact on jazz and on Miles in particular, the extraordinarily brilliant pianist and composer Keith Jarrett and drummer Jack DeJohnette.

The switch to electronics was gradual, like everything else. On *Filles de Kilimanjaro* the quintet's last album togeth-

Miles escorts two friends to Jimi Hendrix's 1970 funeral.
Miles and the rock guitarist had planned to do
a recording session together, but it never happened.

matter of course, the band's personnel changed constantly through the late 1960s and 1970s. Musicians would come in to learn at the University of Miles Davis and then, in most cases, go on to become bandleaders themselves. Among the musicians who came and went (and occasionally came back to play a few sessions) were Wayne Shorter, Herbie Hancock, Ron Carter, Tony Williams, John McLaughlin, Dave Holland, Jack DeJohnette, Al Foster, Keith Jarrett, Larry Young, Joe Zawinul, David Liebman, Bennie Maupin, Reggie Lucas, Dominique Gaumont, Billy Cobham, Harvey Brooks, Sonny Fortune, Carlos Garnett, Lonnie Liston Smith, Billy Hart, Harold Williams, Cedric Lawson, Pete Cosey, Cornell Dupree, John Stubblefield, Mtume, and Azar Lawrence. Miles even brought in three musicians from India—Khalil Balakrishna, Bihari Sharma, and Badal Roy—who tossed their unique bop into the mix.

One of Miles's greatest contributions to music was his mentorship of and generosity with so many young, talented musicians. Many of them might have become successes anyway, but it would have taken longer without Miles's assistance. Indeed, not since Duke Ellington have so many owed so much to one musician.

Offstage and out of the studio, however, Miles's life was problematic. In 1969, an unknown hired gunman tried to kill Miles, missing him as he sat in his Ferrari in Brooklyn. The hit man had been hired by black music promoters who were angry that Miles had been booking his gigs through white promoters. The hit man himself later had an "accident." This episode merely added to the Miles mystique, to the darker side; Miles was called, among other catchy nicknames, Sorcerer and Prince of Darkness.

And in addition to the end of his marriage to Betty Mabry, a long-term affair with a woman named Jackie Battle ended because she could not keep up with his crazed lifestyle. She was incapable of stopping or slowing down his self-destructive behavior—coke, uppers and downers, lots of alcohol. Jackie also could not stop Miles's indiscreet philandering. As in the case of Frances Taylor, Miles regretted her departure from his life.

Another affair, with Marguerite Eskridge, ended for pretty much the same reasons. They had a child, however, a son named Erin. Eskridge didn't extract any palimony from Miles. On the contrary, she whisked the boy away from Miles to Colorado to raise him in a normal environment. Miles somehow managed to remain close to Marguerite and their son.

And then on a concert tour through St. Louis, Miles was haunted by a blast from the past, his former common-law wife, Irene Birth. Irene tore into him in public, attacking Miles as a bad, indifferent father and husband. She blamed him for the way their two sons turned out. One son came back from Vietnam shell-shocked, and the other became a juvenile delinquent and a listless ne'er-do-well. Miles broke down, admitting he had not been there on account of his career—and the drugs, alcohol, and women.

Miles had spent a lot of time ingesting drugs and drink. His excesses led to seemingly insurmountable problems with family, friends, and the law. In his autobiography, Miles described many incidents of police harassment and run-ins with neighbors. It never seemed to have occurred to him that cocaine-induced paranoia might have contributed to these constant hassles and might have made him look suspicious, regardless of his race. Miles's consumption of drugs no doubt exacerbated his long-standing health problems as well. His hip still bothered him, and he developed liver problems, diabetes, and throat nodes; the complications from sickle-cell anemia reappeared. Miles soon looked like a walking corpse.

Another thing that certainly got Miles down must have been the failure of some of his albums to find buyers. The early electric Miles was successful, but beginning with *Live-Evil* (1970) and *On the Corner* (1972), his albums failed to reach any kind of audience, especially the one he wanted most: young blacks. And despite the kind assessment of one critic, Gene Williams of the *Washington Post,* who described Miles's best music of this period as "a dense, electronic rain forest," most of it is nearly unlistenable—a constant, formless barrage of shrieks and wailing.

One exception to this was a track on the *Get Up With It* (1973) album titled "He Loved Him Madly," a mournful, strangely moving dirge dedicated to Duke Ellington (who had just died). The track, painful yet grandiloquent, is dramatic in the way only Miles could be and is characteristically personal. Miles was playing very little trumpet—his throat nodes were bothering him too much at the time—and resorted to the organ, which allowed him to stretch out and create variation upon variation on a skeletal theme. It is, undoubtedly, one of his greatest works.

In any case, deep down Miles must have suspected he was creating garbage, but he really thought that he was still growing, that he was at the forefront of jazz and music in general. Miles had pioneered fusion, no doubt, but the truth is that the children of Miles—Wayne Shorter and Joe Zawinul in Weather Report, Chic Corea in Return to Forever, John McLaughlin with Billy Cobham in Mahavishnu Orchestra, Tony Williams in Lifetime, and Herbie Hancock—were the leaders of fusion jazz. They were the ones who were packing them in, and their music was being listened to around the world. Arguably, the children of Miles, with influences ranging from Europe and the Americas to Africa and Asia and the Middle East, sort of set the world music ball in motion.

The final humiliation was that Miles was now opening for his former pianist, Herbie Hancock, whose *Headhunters* album had gone gold. Miles acted petty about the whole thing, but Hancock, being the gentleman he is, pretended it never happened, and Miles later made something of an apology.

After the Irene Birth blowup, Miles collapsed with nervous exhaustion and had to enter the hospital once again; the hospital was becoming his home away from home. He had bleeding ulcers. When he was released Miles was told to take it easy. So, taking his doctor's advice, Miles did just that, holing up in his West 77th Street apartment for the next five years.

10 The Dark Age

The next five years of Miles Davis's life were shrouded in darkness. As he bluntly put it, "I just took a lot of cocaine [about $500 worth a day at one point] and fucked all the women I could get into my house. I was also addicted to pills, and I was drinking a lot." After nearly 37 years of concentrating on nothing but music, Miles had burnt himself out. His drug and alcohol abuse and sexual escapades had all caught up with him. So while recovering from his collapse, Miles allowed himself to be given completely over to these activities and put aside his brass horn.

Another factor that forced Miles into seclusion was that he again sensed pitying looks directed his way. He was sick and tired, and it was reflected in his music. Miles did not care for the boos, and as much as he hated to admit it, he hated losing touch with his old fans. Hearing "fraud," "sellout," "washed-up," and "has-been" took its toll. Miles did not touch his horn for the next four or five years.

Miles did not lose touch with music, though. Old

friends like Max Roach, Jack DeJohnette, Jackie Battle, Al Foster, Gil Evans, Dizzy, Herbie Hancock, Ron Carter, Tony Williams, Philly Joe Jones, Richard Pryor, and Cicely Tyson came by to tell Miles what was going on beyond his door. They were also checking in to see how he was holding up.

What they saw when they came by must have been a shock. Miles had let himself go. The normally stylish dresser and hipster now seemed indifferent to his appearance. His showplace apartment had literally become a dungeon. It was usually pitch black inside, day and night, because the lights were turned off and the shades were all drawn. Clothes were scattered and heaped everywhere. Dishes piled up in the sink. Garbage was left to accumulate. None of the maids Miles hired would stay for more than a day or two. Sometimes Jackie Battle or Cicely Tyson would try to clean up. Amidst the decay, Miles shambled around the apartment, a drunken, drugged empty shell of a man—drinking, snorting coke, and injecting speedballs (a dangerous combination of cocaine and heroin).

Miles only left his apartment after midnight. He would go to nightclubs on upper Broadway or in Harlem, places where he could sit quietly in the back to do drugs and be left alone. He'd often pick up a woman or two and take her back to his place. Miles went through countless women this way. There were so many that they became a blur. His relationship with his family steadily deteriorated. At one point he was jailed for failing to pay child support for his son Erin.

Finally, Miles was put in the psychiatric ward of Roosevelt Hospital for a few days after a cocaine black-out caused him to punch a woman in the elevator of his building. Miles was so high that he thought he was still in his Ferrari and that the woman was in it, trying to drive it away. His vicious cycle of self-destruction got to the point where he had to decide whether to live or die, and Miles chose to live. He missed the real world, his old friends (they now rarely showed up, except for Max and Diz), and music. Almost as if to remind himself of a glorious, distant past, Miles began to hang pictures of Bird, Trane, Dizzy, and Max around the apartment.

Then George Butler of Columbia Records began showing to check up on Miles. The company had kept paying Miles throughout his quiet time, hoping he would return to recording. They became fast friends, George keeping Miles informed on what was going on outside. Miles would usually ask Butler how various people were getting along, and it wasn't long before they began discussing music and when Miles might want to start playing again. Butler suggested that he could start by just playing at a home first, to get his chops back. Slowly but surely these little encouragements and suggestions got Miles on the right track. He began picking out chords on the piano and, for the first time in years, began thinking and feeling musically again.

Another savior, Cicely Tyson, reentered his life. She had never really left Miles, never really let go, was always there on the fringe, and kept stopping by during his dark period. Cicely cleaned up the apartment as best as she could and got Miles to cut down his drinking and quit drugs completely. She even took it upon herself to see that Miles was getting proper meals. She also got him to stop smoking by threatening to withhold her kisses.

With his health slowly returning, Miles's interest in music grew. Yet another factor in Miles's return from the living dead was Vincent Wilburn, his sister's son. Like Miles, Wilburn had become obsessed with music at an early age, in his case the drums. Miles would sometimes call up his sister just to hear Wilburn play, and when he hit his teens Wilburn started visiting his uncle. He begged Miles to play something, asking if he could jam with him or if Miles

*Miles goes out on the own with
Cicely Tyson. They were married
for seven years.*

would look at this piece he wrote. In a strange yet innocent way, Wilburn reminded Miles of his younger self.

The desire to return to performance was also abetted by Miles's desire to prove his critics wrong once more. In his absence, some critics had written him off completely. They solemnly pronounced that Miles would never return. Miles never paid much attention to critics, but such slights were a challenge. He resolved that he was going to get in shape and make a comeback. In early 1980, Miles called George Butler and told him he had better get ready because Miles was back in town.

Eleven

Miles Smiles

Wanting to play and actually being able to are two different things. When Miles decided to reenter the rat race in 1980, he did not have a band to speak of, except for the formidable Al Foster, the drummer in his last band, and guitarist Pete Cosey. Moreover, not having played for five years left Miles without chops. It would take time to regain his embouchure and to get back into the physical condition to play as he had.

Putting together a band, though, was not as difficult as it first seemed. During his period of seclusion, Miles had kept in touch with a few musician friends, including his one-time reed man, David Liebman. Liebman put Miles on to Bill Evans, a young tenor/soprano saxophonist. Vincent Wilburn, Miles's nephew, brought in some friends from Chicago: Randy Hall, Robert Irving, Felton Crews, Marcus Miller, and Barry Finnerty. In short order, though, the band thinned out to Miller, Evans, Foster, Minno Cinelu on percussion, and guitarist Mike Stern (later replaced by John Scofield).

Rehearsal came first, then the road. It got leaked that Miles and his new band were playing secret dates in Boston, testing the waters before hitting the big-time, New York. The dates sold out in a matter of hours and, though Miles was not what he used to be, his return was warmly and wildly received. In his autobiography, Miles tells an anecdote of how a small black man sitting in a wheelchair in the front row, a victim of cerebral palsy, was so moved by Miles's playing that he reached up, shaking like a leaf, to touch the bell of his trumpet, a gesture of benediction. Miles was so touched that he nearly lost it. He needed that, the approval, the applause, the gesture of solidarity.

Miles's approach to performance changed this time round. He lightened up, introducing the band and announcing numbers now and then. He even chatted and joked with the audience. Age had mellowed him somewhat, a welcome surprise for fans and critics alike.

Nevertheless, the critics whined about Miles being a shadow of his former self. Miles ignored them. What bothered Miles was the crude, common way his sidemen were lambasted. With the exception of Al Foster, a tour veteran, the rest—Miller, Cinelu, Stern, and Evans—were young and impressionable, anxious to make names for themselves, and all too eager to please. The vehemence with which they were attacked was not just unsettling but demoralizing. A wise leader, Miles took aside his young charges and reassured them. Miles told them that the critics were attacking him, as they had always done. He reminded the younger musicians that the critics had also attacked Bird, Diz, Trane, and anybody else who was a bit different. Years later the critics loved their music, Miles explained, but never when they were creating it. His little pep talk made the band much closer, and they improved musically. The band's first album, *The Man with the Horn* (1980), was savaged in the press but sold 100,000 copies very quickly. Overseas, their concerts were sell-outs. In Japan, Miles and the band were paid $700,000 for eight shows.

Miles's private life also took on a new dimension. In the fall of 1981, he married Cicely Tyson, who had stuck by him through darkness and light. When Miles discovered that he was diabetic, Cicely helped him quit alcohol. When he suffered a stroke in 1981, shortly after their marriage, she nursed him and helped him get movement back in his right hand. She could do nothing about his mysterious loss of hair, which was probably a result of the combination of all the prescription drugs he was on and stress due to his health.

Despite this, it was not a happy marriage. Miles and Cicely were simply incompatible, and they went through an ugly divorce in 1988. A number of unpleasant incidents highlighted the marriage. She would come on tour with the band, bring along a friend, and according to Miles, treat the roadies as if they were her personal servants. Several of the roadies would quit each time out. When Miles was playing with B. B. King at the Beacon Theater in New York, he and Cicely had a nasty argument right before he went onstage. She jumped on his back, began pounding him, and for good measure she pulled off his hair weave. Miles had to play without his rug.

Another time Cicely was invited to the White House for a dinner given in honor of the singer Ray Charles. Miles did not much care for ceremonies or politicians, but Ray was a friend so he went along. Miles met Nancy and Ronald Reagan and surprisingly found them charming and kind. Everything was going smoothly until they were in a car going to the Kennedy Center for the Performing Arts for the musical segment of the evening. In the limousine, a white woman, trying to be polite, said to Miles, "I know your mammy's proud of you running down to meet the President." Miles ripped into her, "Listen, my mother ain't no motherfucking mammy, you hear what I'm telling you! That word is out of style and people don't use it anymore. My mother was more elegant and proper than you could ever be, and my father was a doctor. So don't you ever say anything like that to a black person anymore, you hear what I'm saying to you?" The woman, who probably meant no harm, apologized, but Cicely gave Miles a hard time about it later on. When they got to the Kennedy Center, Miles was seated next to a big politician's wife. She began asking him rather pointed questions about jazz; probably she only wanted to hear herself talk. She wanted to know why jazz wasn't given its due in the United States. Miles replied:

Jazz is ignored here because the white man likes to win at everything. White people like to see other white people win just like you do and they can't win when it comes to jazz and the blues because black people created this. And so when we play in Europe, white people over there appreciate us because they know who did what and they will admit it. But most white Americans won't.

This made the woman indignant, and she shot back, "Well, what have you done that's so important in your life? Why are you here?" "Well," Miles snapped, "I've changed music five or six times, so I guess that's what I've done and I guess I don't believe in playing just white compositions. Now, you tell me what have you done of any importance other than be white, and that ain't important to me, so tell me what your claim to fame is?" Miles tore into Tyson afterward for dragging him to inane society functions. Soon they were living apart.

Miles and the band continued to prosper, regardless of the personnel. Al Foster, Miles's stalwart drummer, left and

*Miles plays during a 1987 concert in Israel.
When Miles returned to active performing in 1985 after
a ten-year absence, he kept exploring new
ideas and sounds.*

was replaced by Miles's nephew Vincent Wilburn. Wilburn was eventually fired because he could not protect the beat. The rocker Mike Stern was replaced by the brilliant John Scofield, who in turn was succeeded by the dynamic Foley. Bill Evans left of his own accord and was followed by Bob Berg and, in one studio session, Branford Marsalis. The steady Marcus Miller traded his bass for a producer's hat and was replaced by Darryl Jones who was in for about a year before he left to play with the rock musician Sting.

Miles's musical samplings were no less varied than before, as evidenced in his records. From the slightly affected sound of *The Man with the Horn*, to the pop/funk sounds of *Star People* (1982) and *Decoy* (1983), to the avant-garde musical compositions of the Danish composer Palle Mikkelborg on *Aura* (1989), to a cover of Cyndi Lauper's "Time after Time," Miles was all over the map. He even got around to rap, recording with Easy Mo Bee.

Now and then in concert, Miles would play a standard, such as "My Man's Gone Now" from George Gershwin's *Porgy and Bess*, often in memory of such departed friends and colleagues as Charles Mingus, Thelonious Monk, and his old piano player Bill Evans, who died of complications from heroin addiction.

Although Miles may have felt unappreciated at home, he garnered many honors here and abroad. In 1983, the Black Music Association, in cooperation with Radio City Music Hall, organized a celebration called Miles Ahead for him at Radio City Music Hall. Among the guests were Herbie Hancock, J. J. Johnson, Ron Carter, George Benson, Jackie McLean, Tony Williams, Philly Joe Jones, and many others. Bill Cosby hosted the event, and Quincy Jones arranged the music and conducted the orchestra. When the president of Fisk University awarded Miles an honorary degree, Miles said thanks and stepped off the podium. He wasn't much for speeches.

Shining Trumpets: A History of Jazz (New York: Da Capo, 1975) by Rudy Blesh has to be the most foolish book on this list. A "trad" fan, Blesh hates anything that came after 1940 and a lot that happened before, such as Duke Ellington's experimental combos or Fletcher Henderson's hard swing. For Blesh, jazz never recovered from the demise of Satchmo's Hot Five. Although Miles is an anathema to Blesh, he reserves his greatest scorn for the boppers.

Jazz People (New York: Da Capo, 1993) by Dan Morgenstern has lots of wonderful, up-close-and-personal pictures and a serviceable text.

I also drew on material from books written by or about artists who were close to Miles, such as Dizzy Gillespie's revealing autobiography *To Be or Not to Bop* (New York: Doubleday, 1993); a videotape, *John Coltrane: The Coltrane Legacy*; and the African writer E. B. Dongala's wonderful book of essays and vignettes, *Jazz et vin de palme*, which contains a memoir of Coltrane.

The late *New Yorker* critic and composer Virgil Thomson had some interesting opinions about jazz, which you can read in *Virgil Thomson* (New York: Da Capo, 1977).

Finally, like anyone else mad about jazz, I love good liner notes. The late Ralph J. Gleason, who wrote the notes for *Bitches Brew* and many other recordings, stands out. These, plus magazine and newspaper articles too numerous to mention here, proved invaluable.

For Further Reading

Chambers, Jack. *Milestones I and II: The Music and Times of Miles Davis*. Toronto: University of Toronto Press.

Cole, Bill. *Miles Davis: The Early Years*. New York: Da Capo, 1994.

Davis, Miles, with Quincy Troupe. *Miles*. New York: Touchstone, 1990.

Feather, Leonard. *The Encyclopedia of Jazz*. New York: Da Capo, 1984.

———. *From Satchmo to Miles*. New York: Da Capo, 1987.

Frankl, Ron. *Miles Davis*. Broomall, PA: Chelsea House, 1996.

Gillespie, Dizzy, and Al Fraser Long. *To Be or Not to Bop*. New York: Doubleday, 1993.

Hentoff, Nat. *Jazz Is*. New York: Limelight Editions, 1984.

Long, Daryl. *Miles Davis for Beginners*. New York: Writers and Readers, 1992.

Williams, Richard. *Miles Davis: The Man in the Green Shirt*. New York: Holt, 1993.

Selected Discography

Because a complete discography is well-nigh impossible—even as you read this, another Miles CD is probably being released (there are thousands of hours of music in Sony/Columbia's vaults)—I have selected the essential recordings from all periods of Miles's career.

Early Miles is best heard on the recordings of Charlie Parker, of which there are many, and of Billy Eckstine, which unfortunately are harder to find. Miles can also be found on the late 1940s to early 1950s Columbia recordings of Sarah Vaughn as an accompanyist. Small combo works from this period thankfully are becoming easier to find, thanks to reissues, and those from Atlantic Records are the best. *Collector's Items*, a two-record set, is a treasure that includes sessions with such giants as Bird (who plays tenor on one cut!), Mingus, Monk, Sonny Rollins, Klook, Art Blakey, Tommy Flanagan, John Coltrane, Walter Bishop, Jackie McLean, Horace Silber, and others. *Collector's Items* is now out of print, but its contents—such as "Blueing," "In

Your Own Sweet Way," "Nature Boy," and others—can be found elsewhere.

All the great 1950s quintet and sextet recordings are readily available, including *Walkin'* (Prestige, 1954), *Steamin'* (Prestige, 1956), *Cookin'* (Prestige, 1956), *Relaxin'* (Prestige, 1956), *'Round About Midnight* (Columbia, 1955), *Milestones* (Columbia, 1958), *Kind of Blue* (Columbia, 1959), all the way up to the Carnegie Hall concerts with Gil Evans in 1961. *'58 Sessions: Stella by Starlight* is a must, if only for its definitive version of "Love for Sale" (with Coltrane swinging à la Lester Young) and the live takes on the other side, which show the band really cooking.

The collaborations with Gil Evans—*Birth of the Cool* (EMI/Capitol, 1950), *Miles Ahead* (Columbia, 1957) *Sketches of Spain* (Columbia, 1960), and *Porgy and Bess* (Columbia, 1958)—are widely available and worth owning. *Miles Ahead* (Columbia, 1957), Miles and Gil's Ellington-inspired masterpiece and my special favorite, is one of the greatest jazz recordings ever.

There are notable interesting recordings that pre-date the second great quintet, notably *Seven Steps to Heaven*, *E.S.P* (Columbia, 1965), and, above all, *My Funny Valentine* (Columbia, 1964), a live concert recorded just before the underrated tenor George Coleman left the band. The creative tension on that last night pushed the band to amazing heights, no more so than on "I Thought About You," where Coleman's masterfully crafted solo is, for me anyway, heartwrenching. The actual second quintet, with Wayne Shorter replacing Coleman, yields up such riches as *Sorcerer*, *Cookin' at the Plugged Nickel* (a brilliant live recording, especially the opening track "If I Were a Bell"), *Miles Smiles* (Columbia, 1966), *Miles in the Sky* (Columbia, 1968), *Filles de Kilimanjaro* (Columbia, 1968), and *Nefertiti* (CBS, 1967).

Miles's electric phase starts off well but ends up a dirge.

Highpoints include *In a Silent Way* (Columbia, 1969; it features the quintet plus Chick Corea, Joe Zawinul, Dave Holland, John McLaughlin, and Jack DeJohnette), the seminal *Bitches Brew* (Columbia, 1969), *Get Up With It* (Columbia, 1970; it contains "He Loved Him Madly," Miles's mournful elegy to Duke Ellington), and *Agharta* (CBS, 1975).

Miles's final period, 1980–91, my least favorite and his most blatantly commercial, is not, however, entirely without merit. *The Man with the Horn* (CBS, 1980; "Backseat Betty" is a real goer), *Aura*, and his last recording, *Miles & Quincy Live at Montreux*, the Gil Evans–inspired collaboration with Quincy Jones (posthumously released) bear relistening.

See you in the record shop.

Index

Adderley, Julian "Cannon-
    ball," 80, 85–88, 89, 102,
    110, 111
Aura, 130

Bebop jazz , 12, 23, 41, 47,
    52, 53, 61, 76, 80, 107
Billy Eckstine's Big Band, 26,
    32–33, 55, 61, 62, 66
Birth, Irene (first wife),
    27–28, 39, 41, 48, 52, 67,
    68, 117, 119
Birth of the Cool, 14, 60, 61,
    66–67, 85, 89
Bitches Brew, 112
Blakey, Art, 67, 71, 75, 93,
    100, 104

Carter, Ron, 100, 101, 103,
    104, 111, 113, 116, 121, 130
Chambers, Paul, 80, 81,
    82–83, 85, 87, 94, 100
Clarke, Kenny "Klook," 12,
    43, 62, 64, 66, 76, 100

Cocaine, 55, 66, 67, 81, 106,
    117, 120, 121
Coleman, Ornette, 94–96, *95*,
    101
Coltrane, John, 47, 49, 80–84,
    82–83, 85, 87, 88, 89, 93,
    101, 102, 103, 106–107,
    110, 111, 113, 122, 126,
    132
Columbia Records, 79, 100,
    109, 112, 122
Cool jazz, 12, 59–60, 74, 76
Corea, Chick, 111, 112, 114,
    118

Davis, Cleota Henry (moth-
    er), 14, 19, 22, 23, 24, 26,
    27, 28, 32, 99, 128
Davis, Dorothy, (sister),
    21–22, 32, 71, 77
Davis, Miles Dewey, II,
    (father), 17, *18*, 19, 20, 21,
    22, 23, 24, 26, 27, 28, 32,
    43–44, 70, 71–73, 99, 128

About the Author

As a teenage trumpet player growing up in the South, George R. Crisp discovered the music of Miles Davis in a secondhand record shop owned by a retired big-band drummer. Although the world was spared yet another Miles imitator, it was not spared another writer, as Mr. Crisp took up writing, first in art school, then at Columbia University. He has written for many publications, including *Opera News*, *Art Review* (UK), the *San Francisco Chronicle Book Review*, the *New York Observer*, and the *International Herald Tribune*. Mr. Crisp divides his time between London and New York.